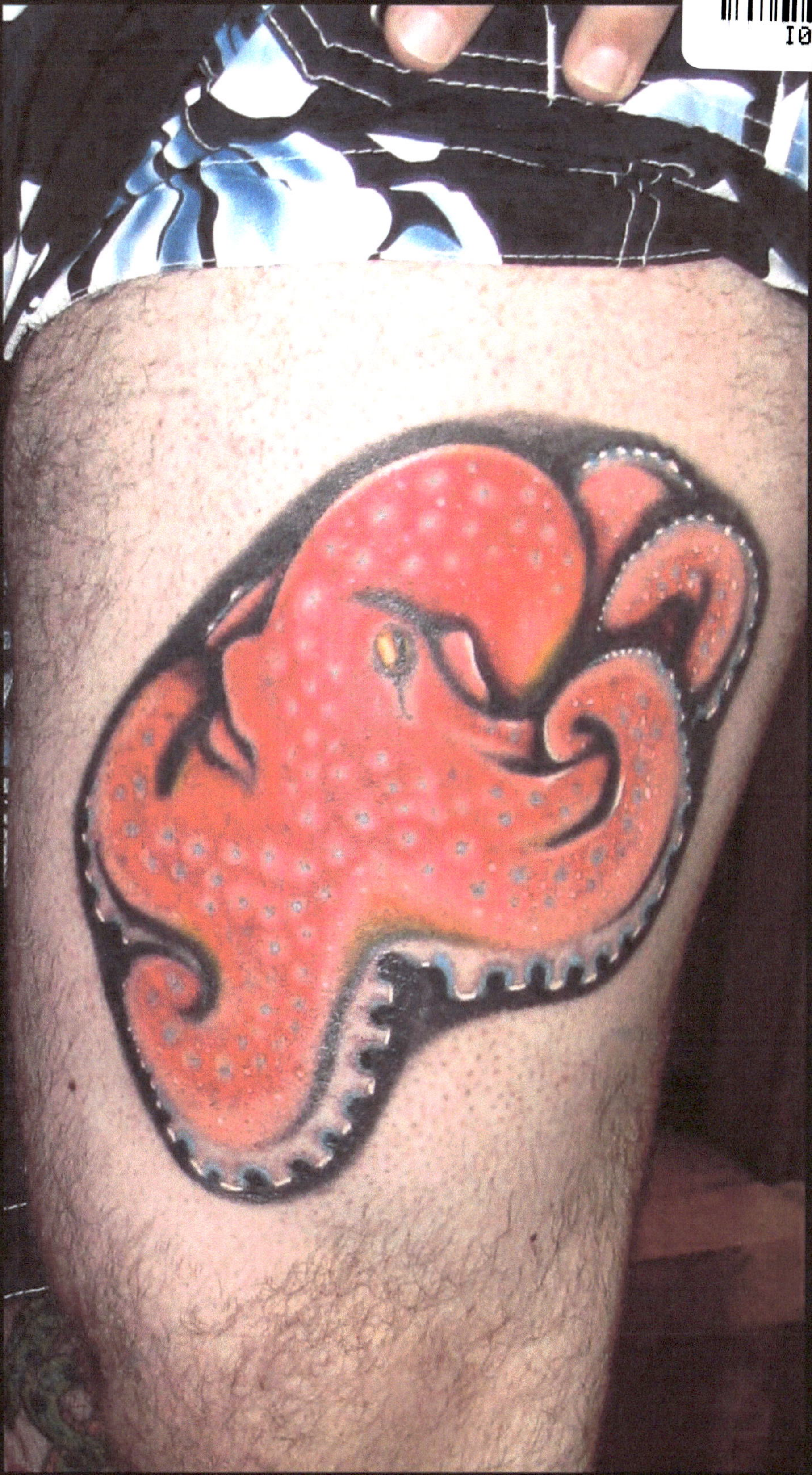

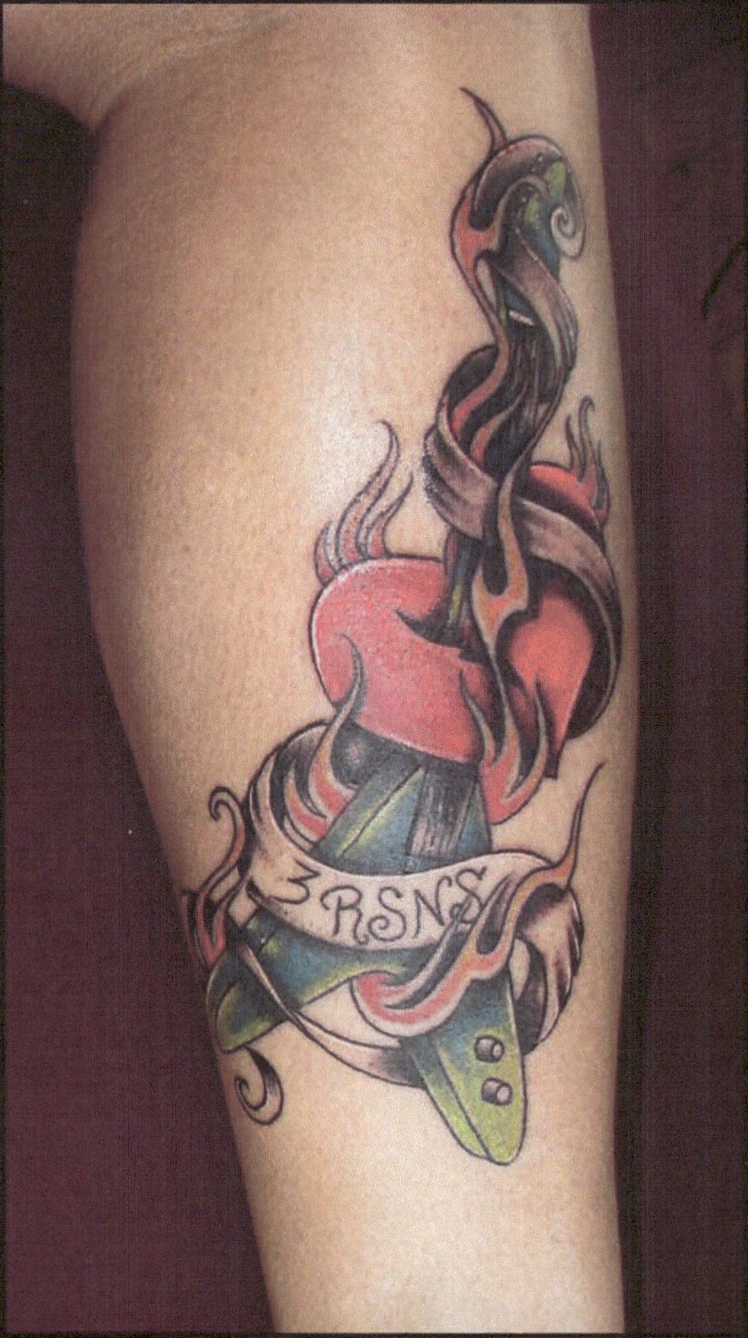
3RSNS

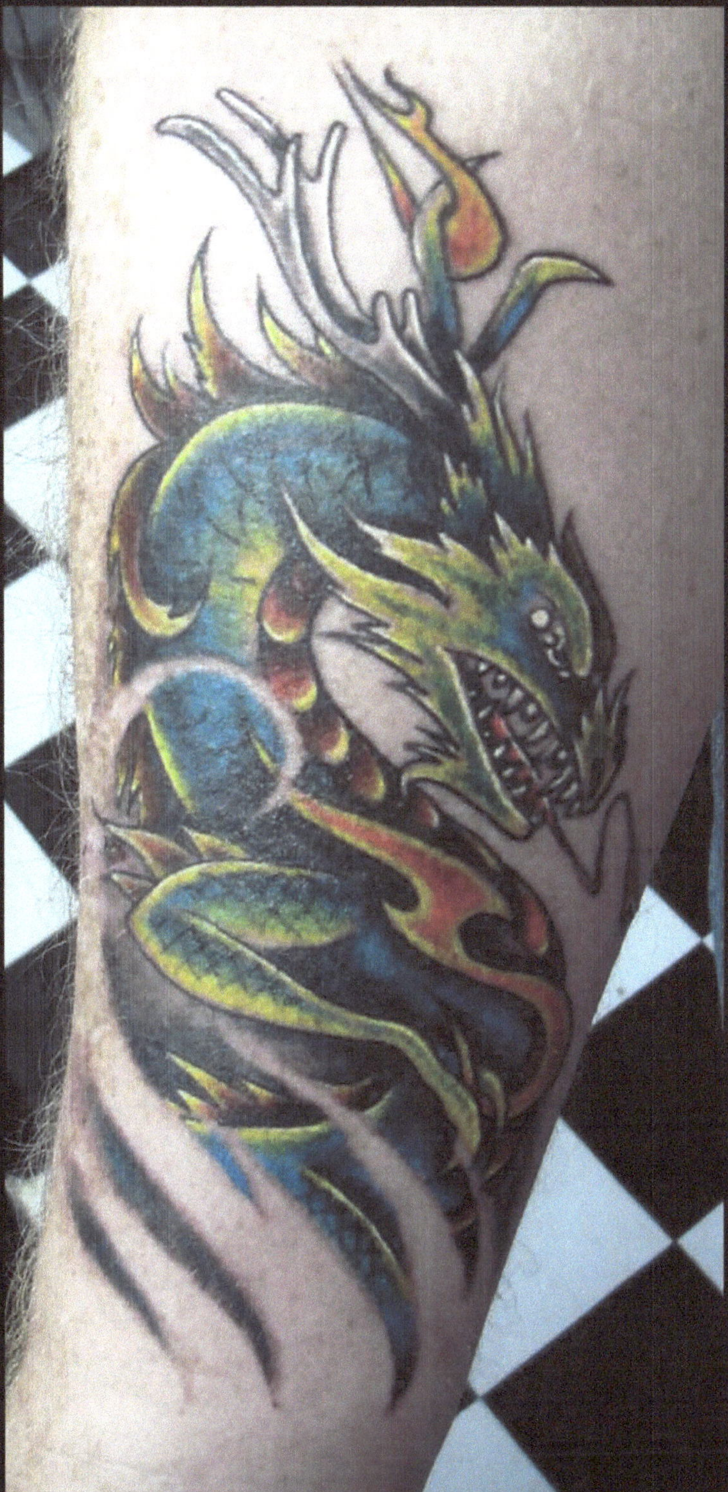

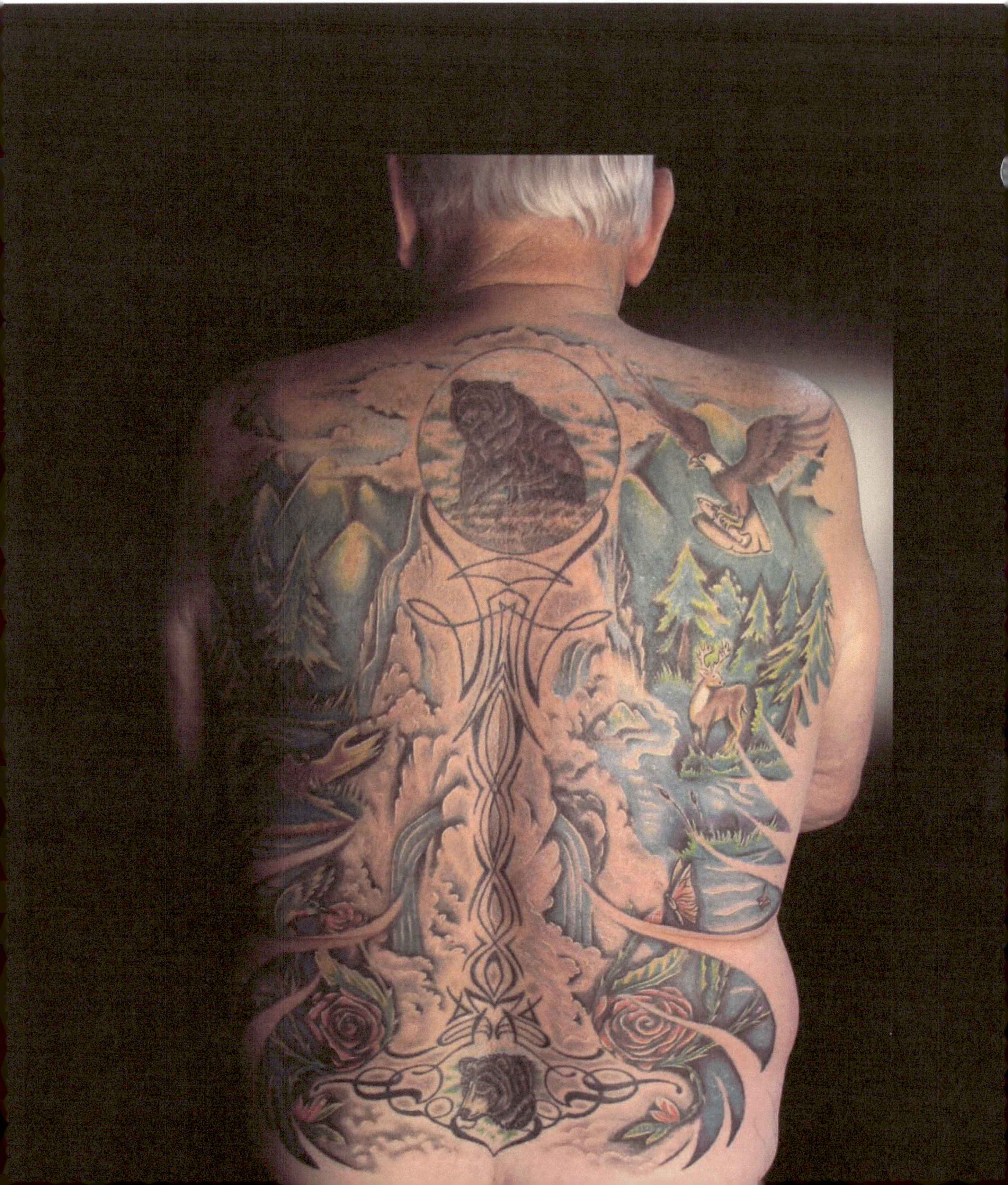

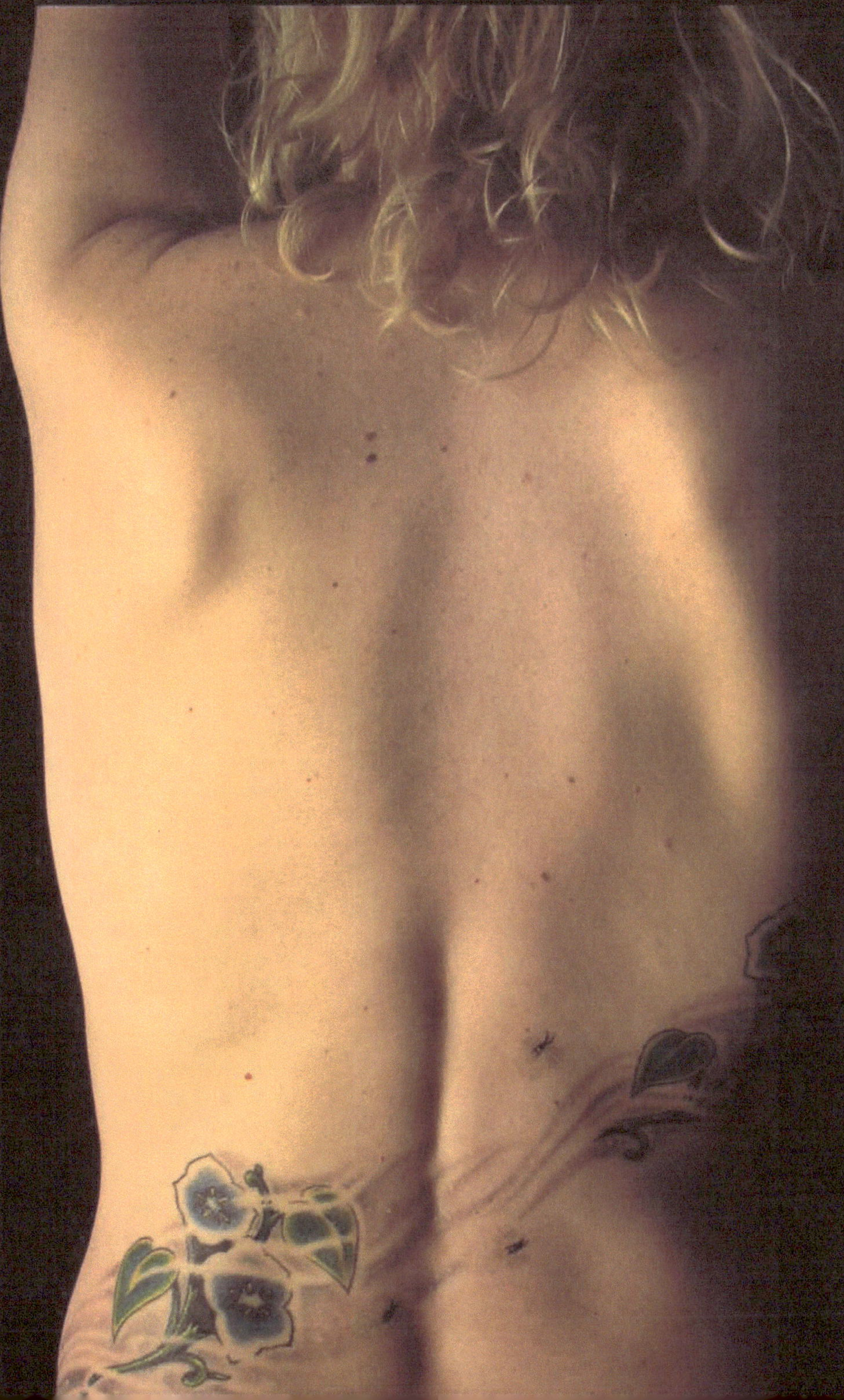

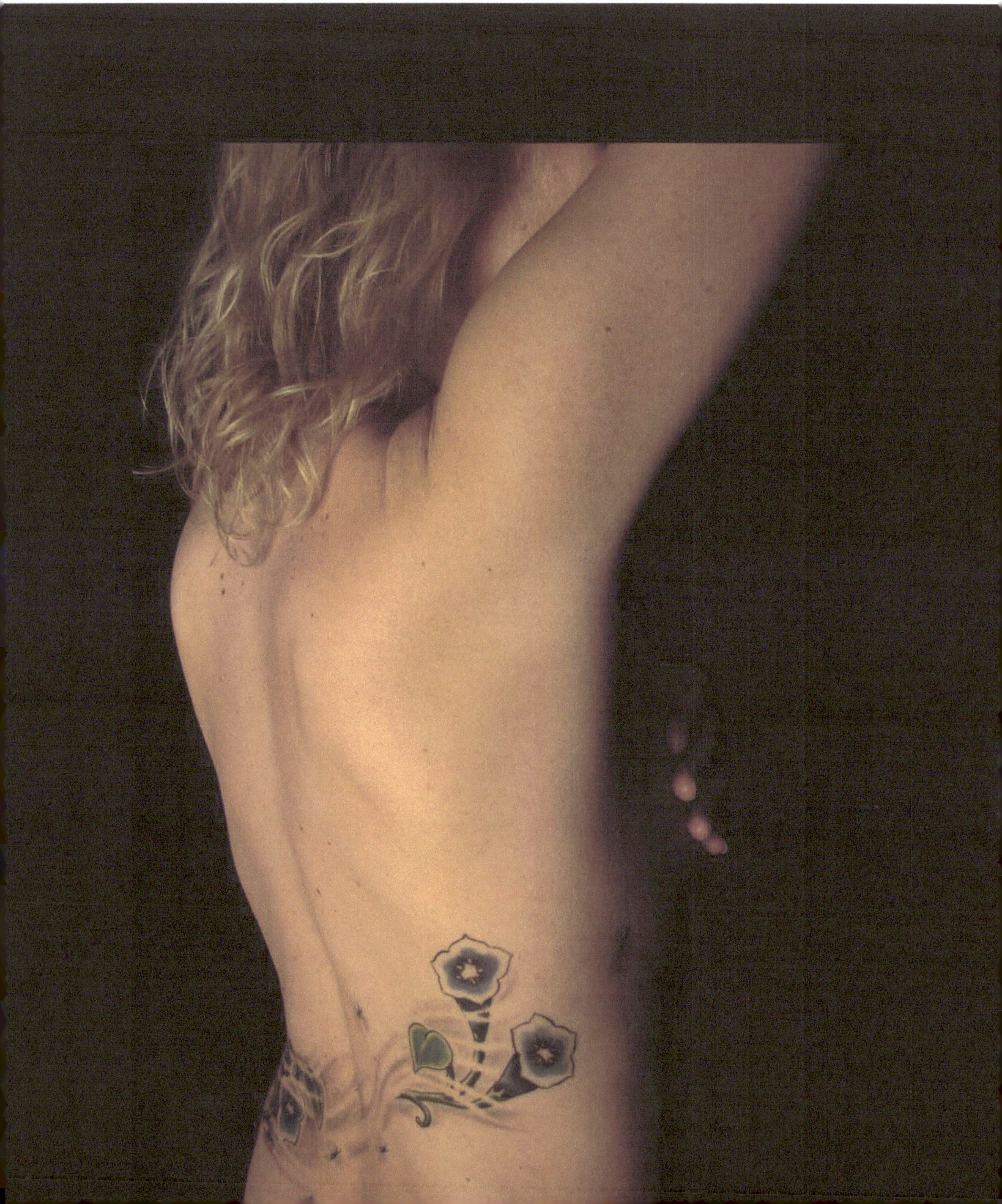

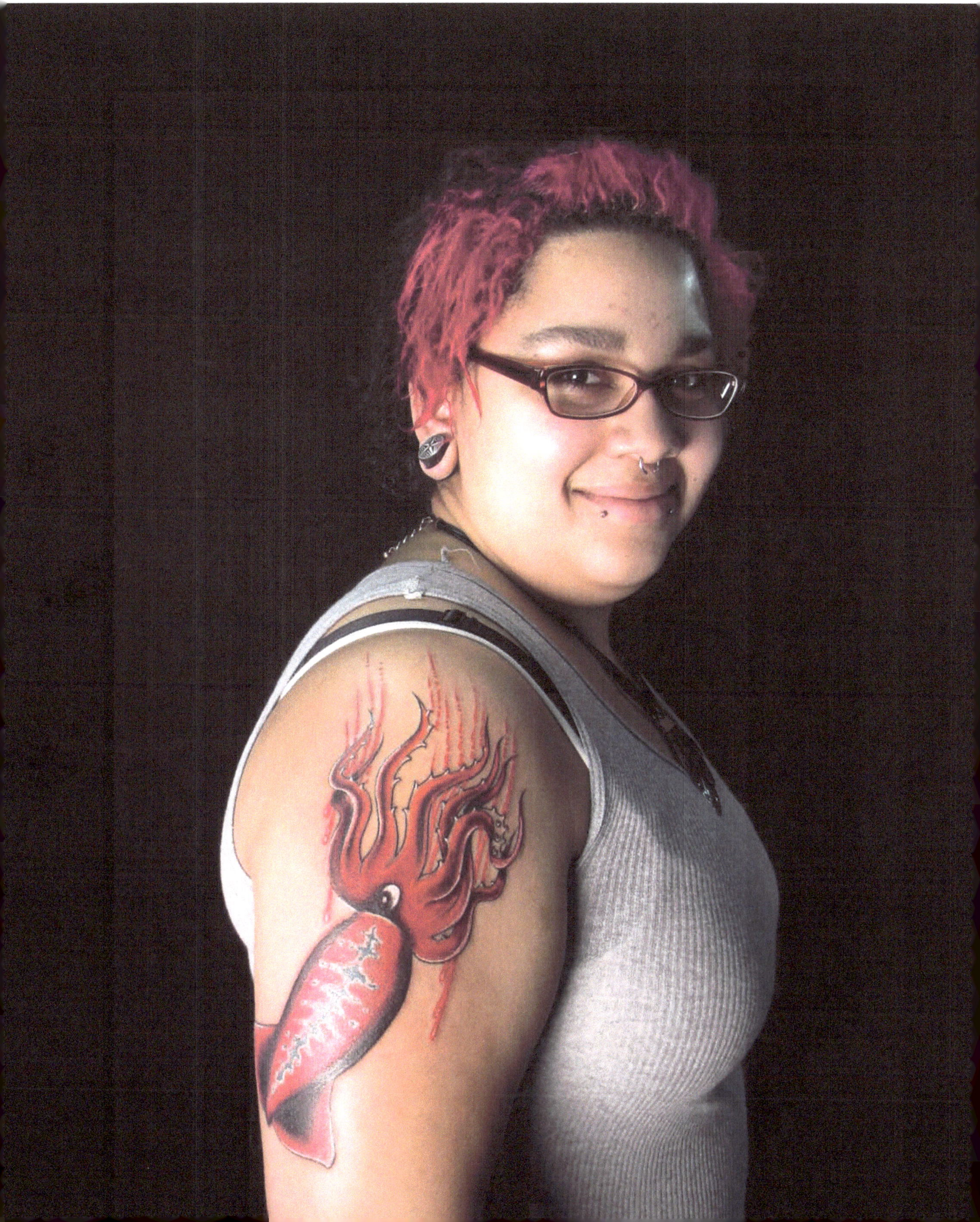

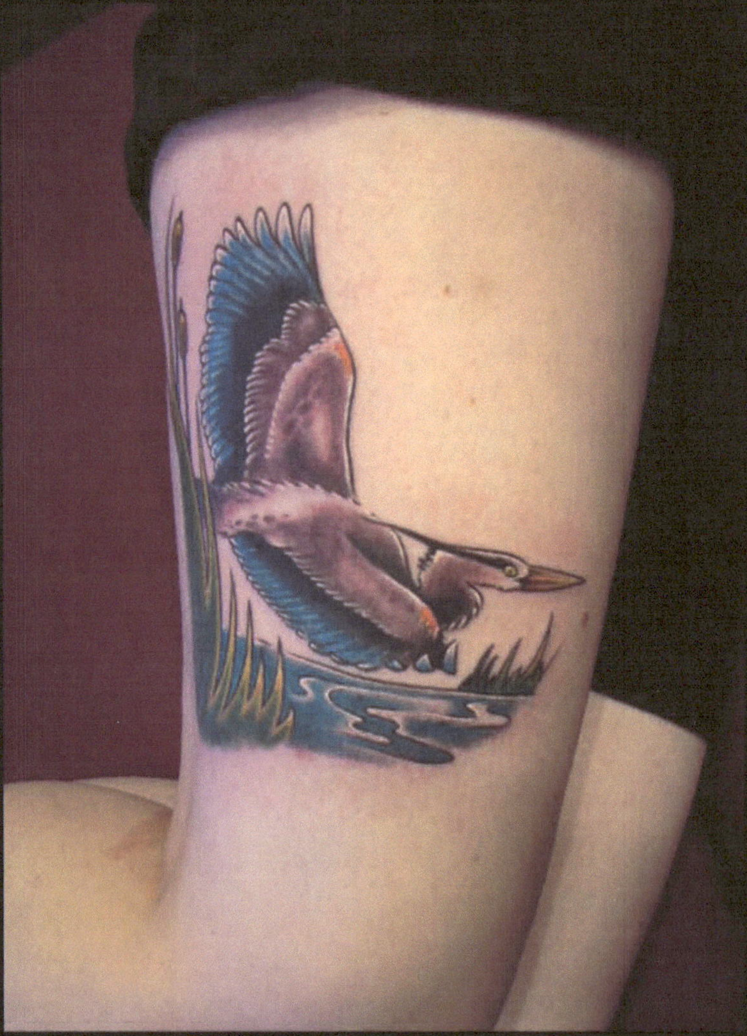

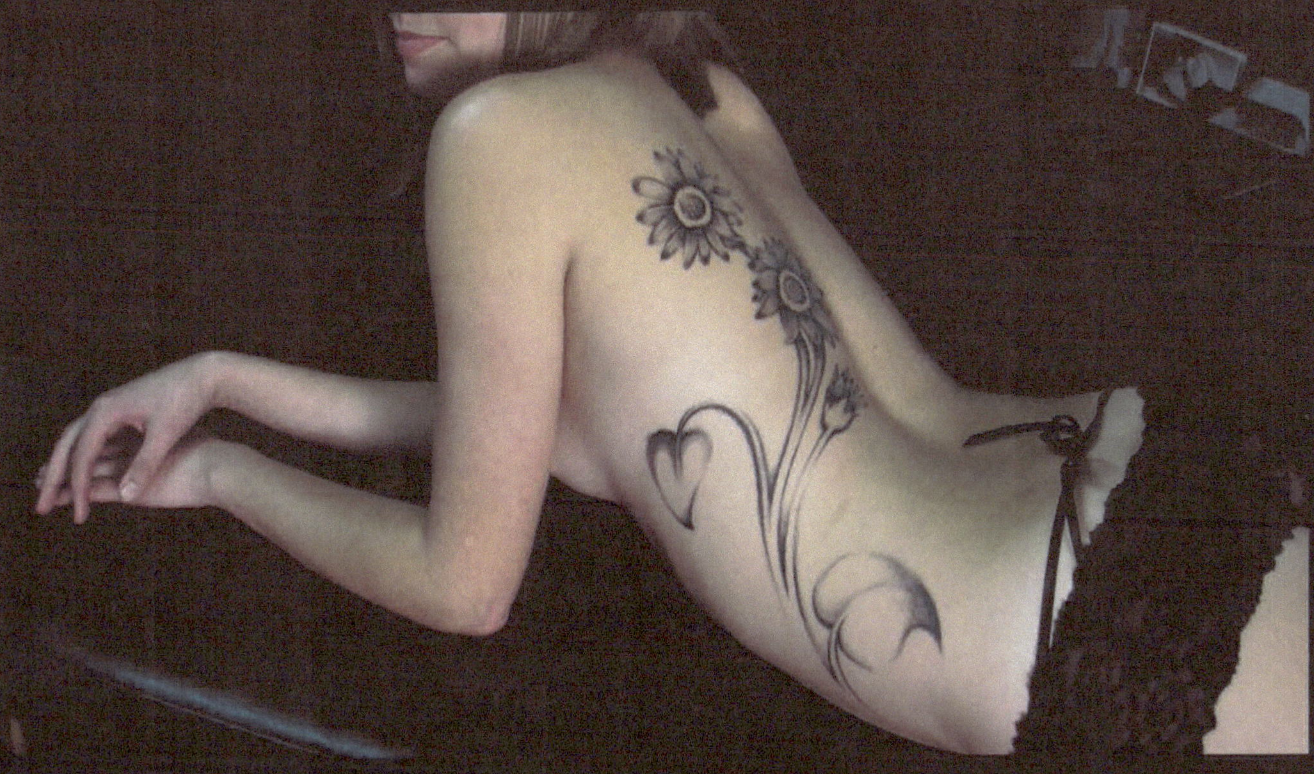

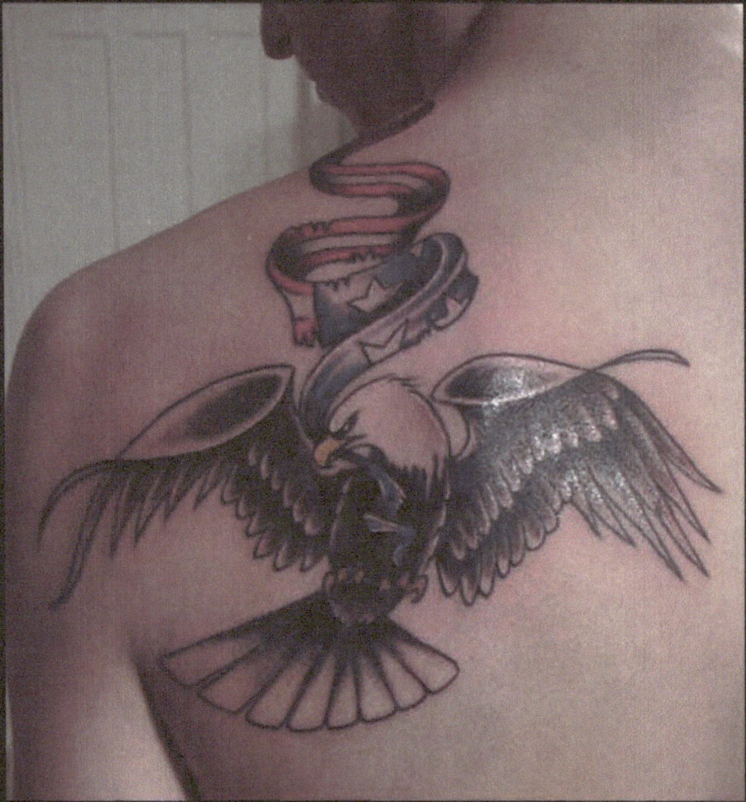

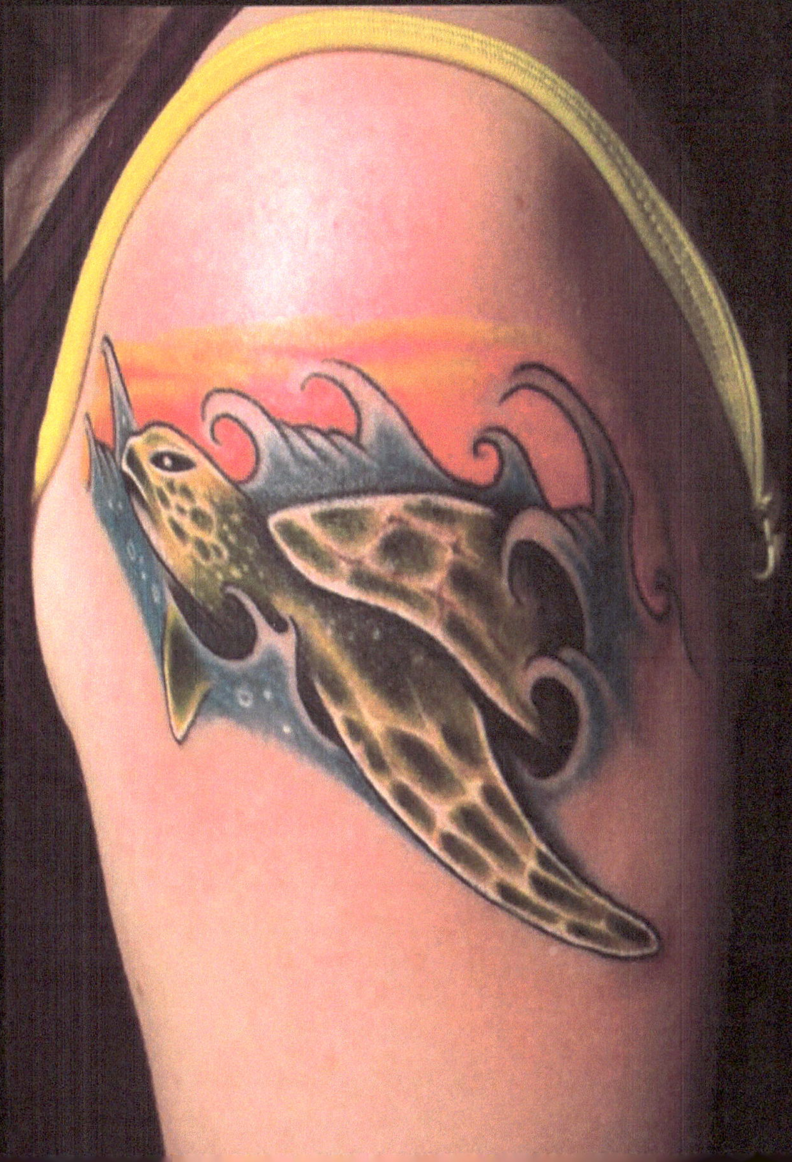

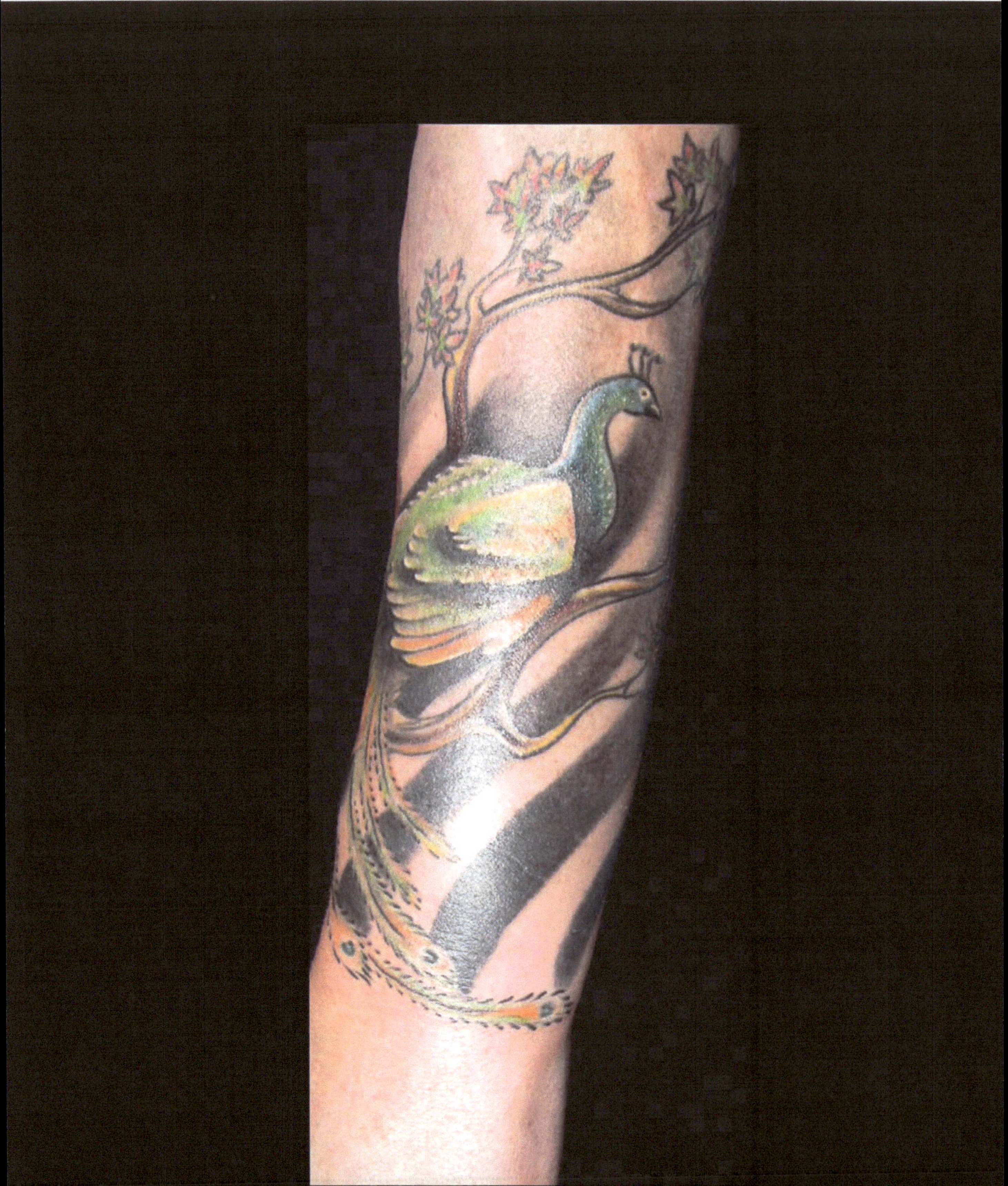

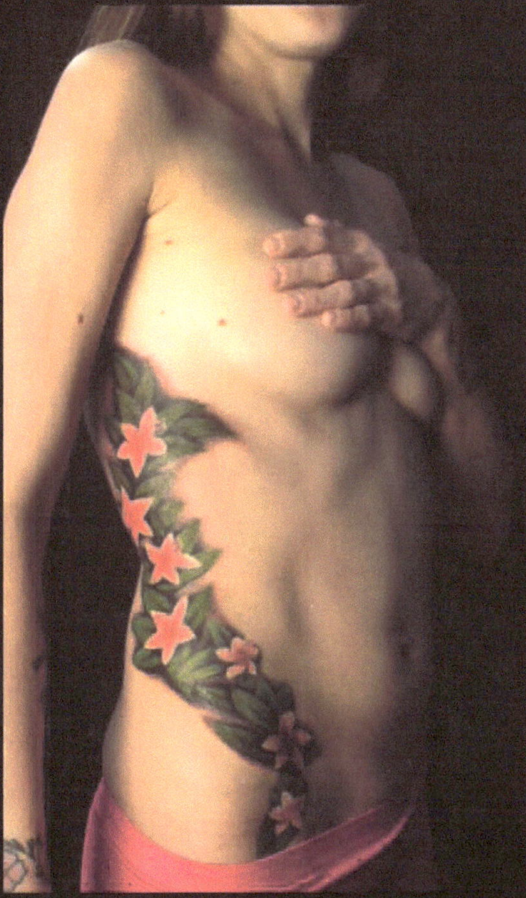
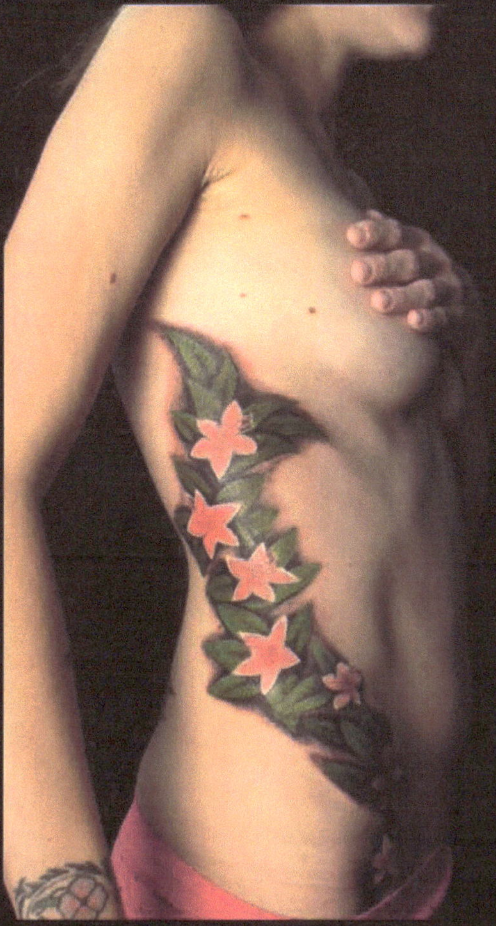

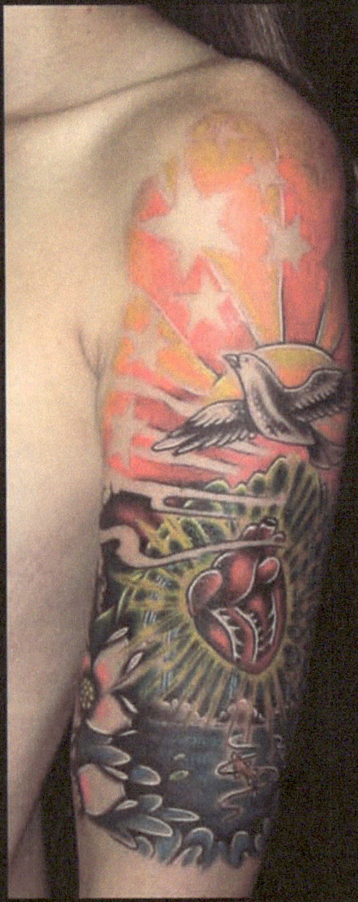
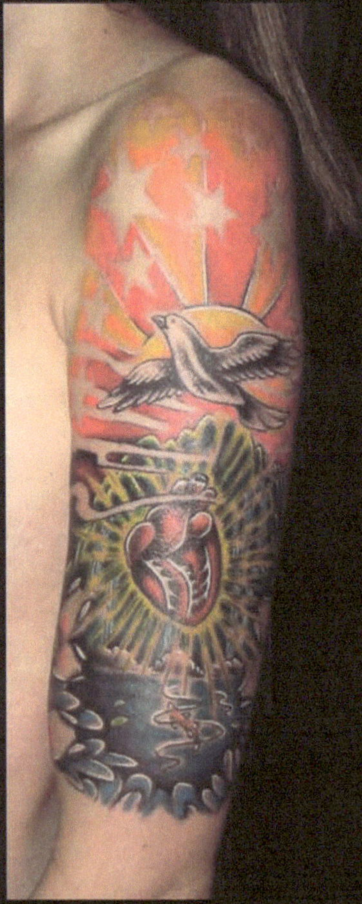
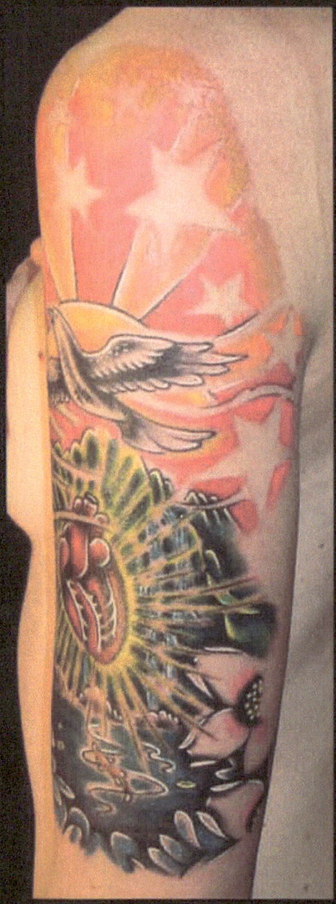

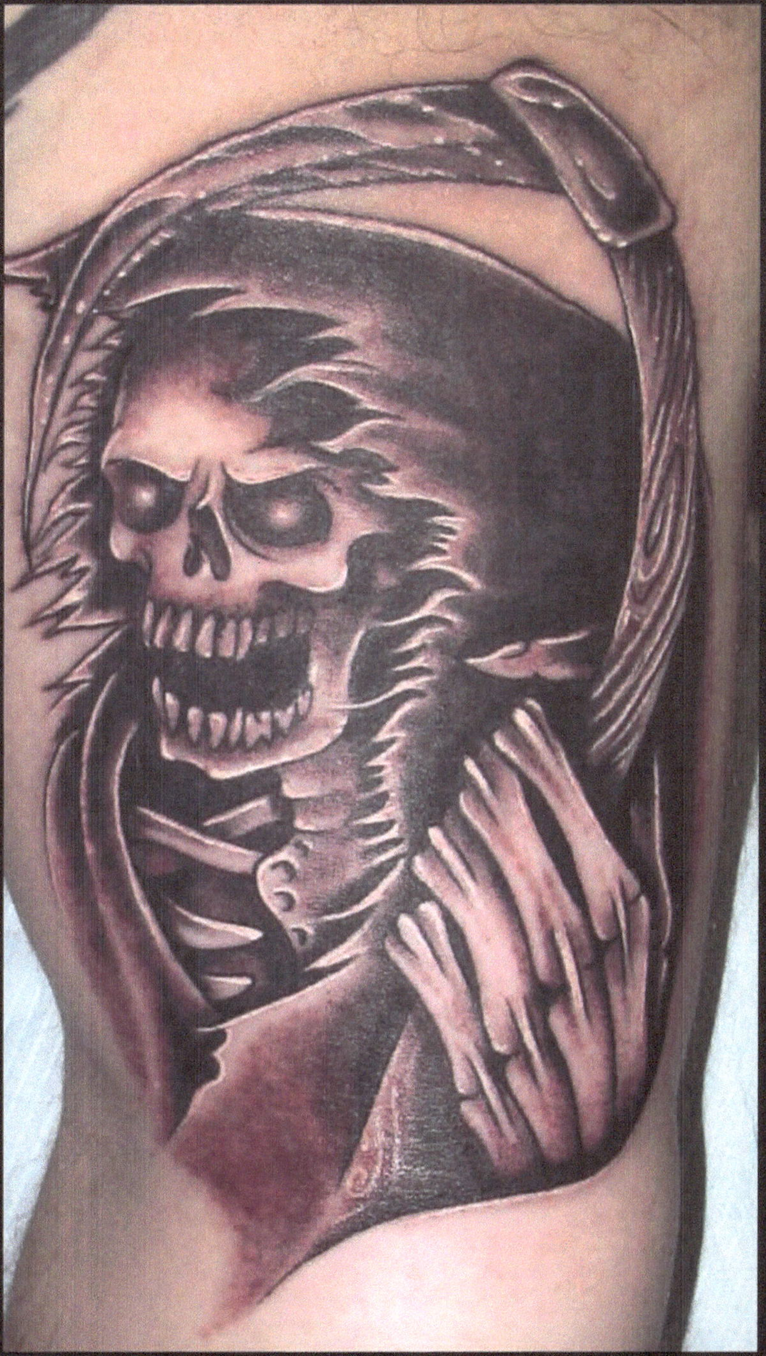

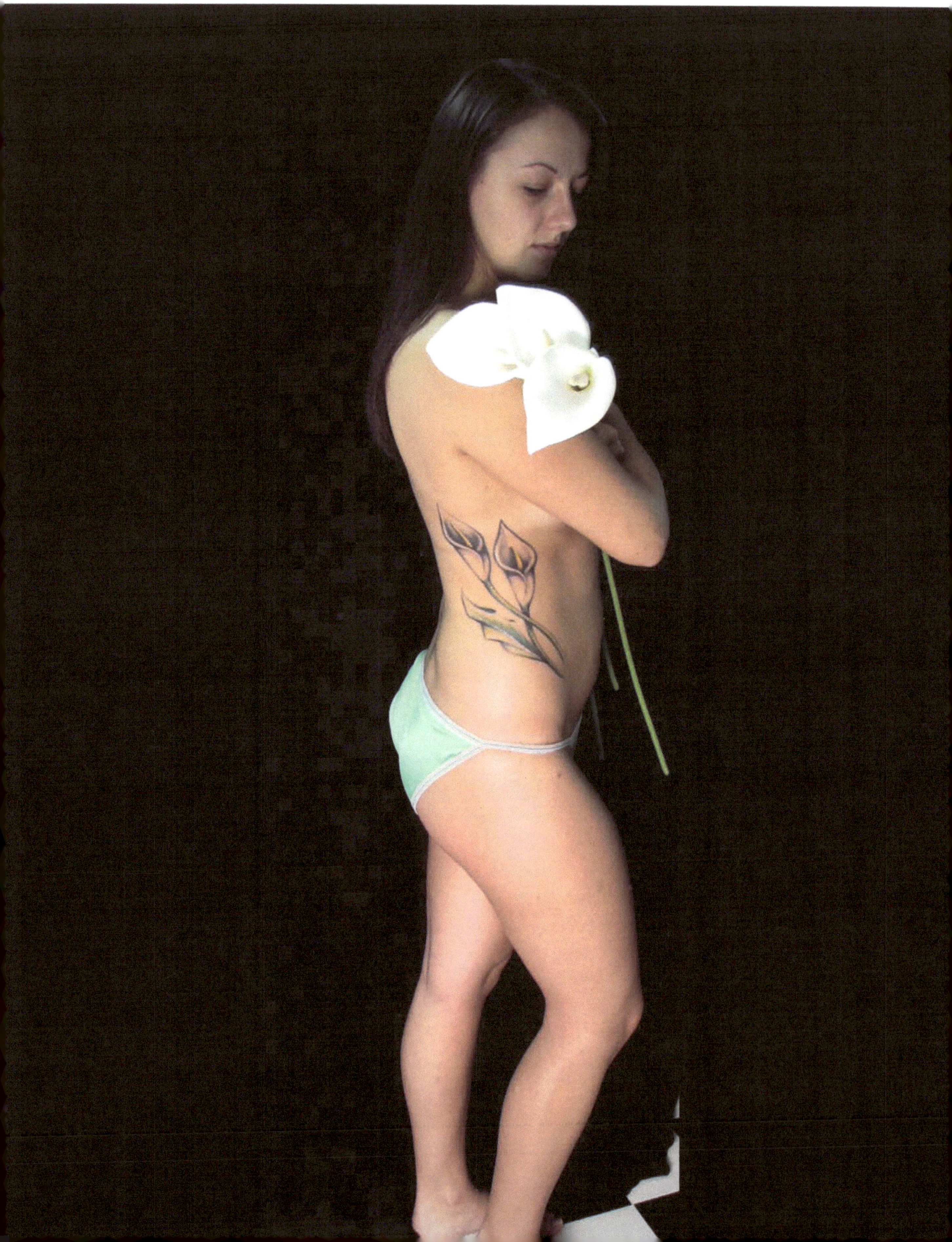

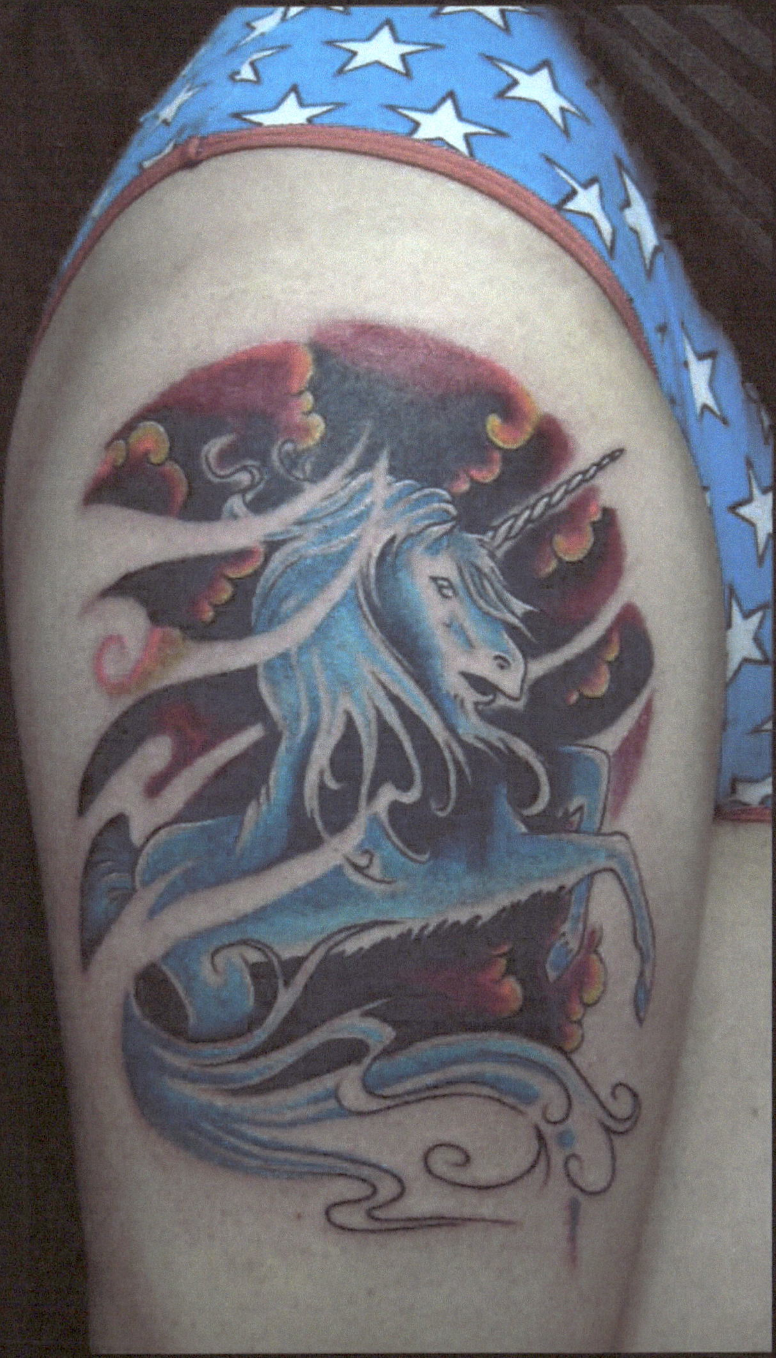

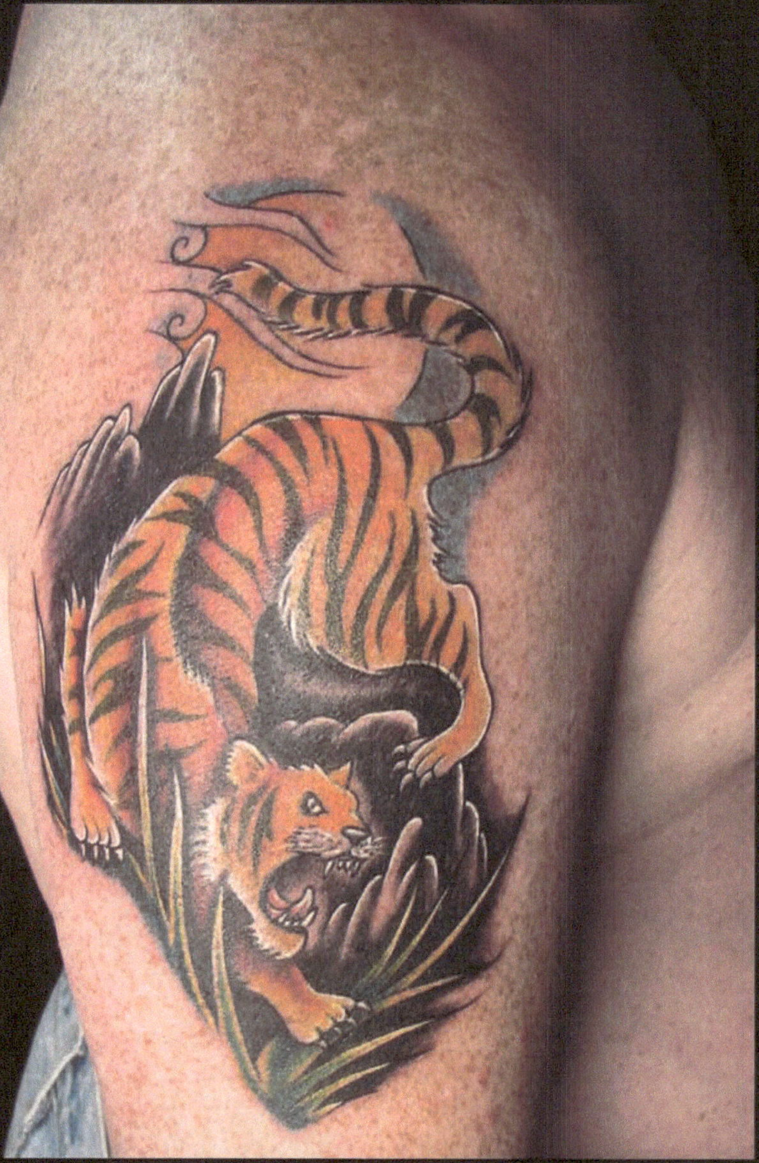

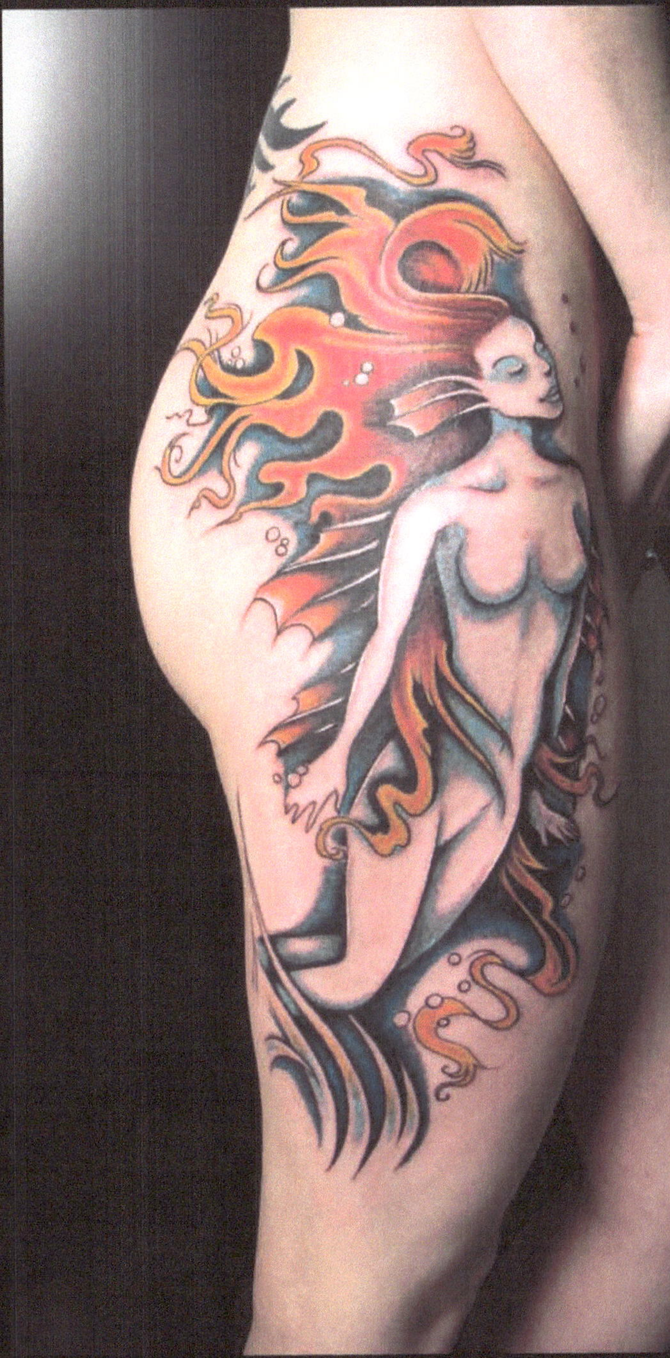

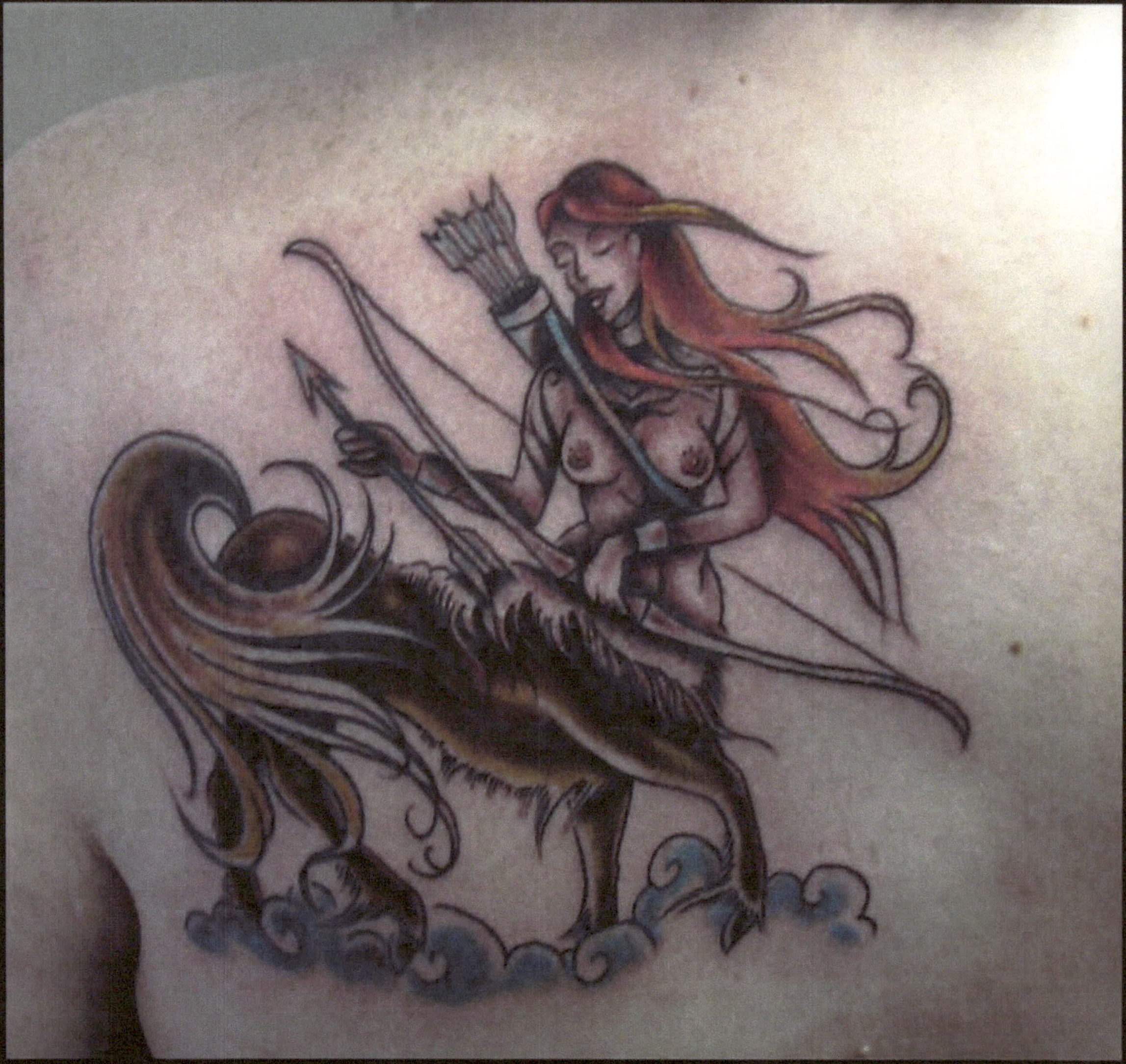

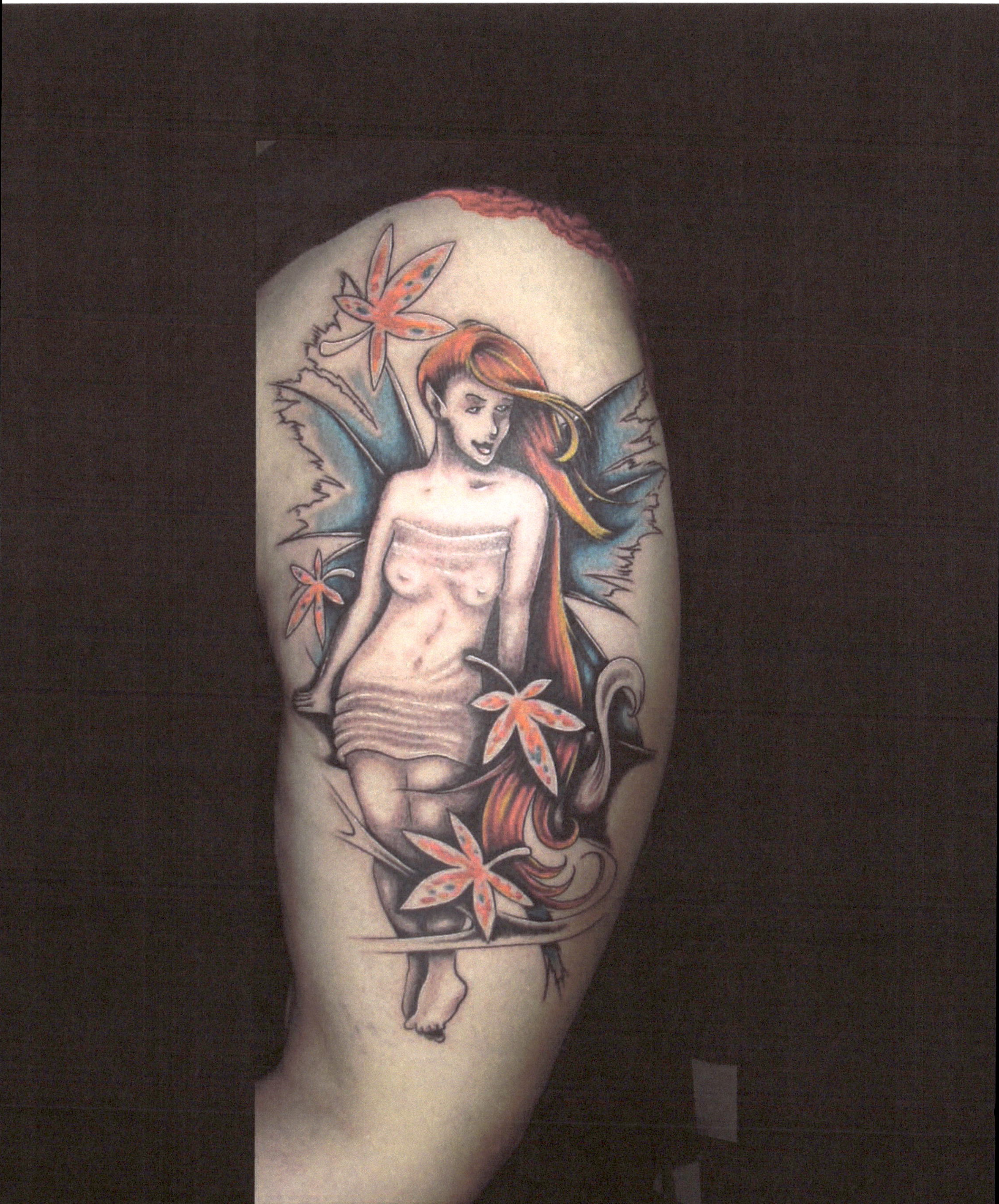

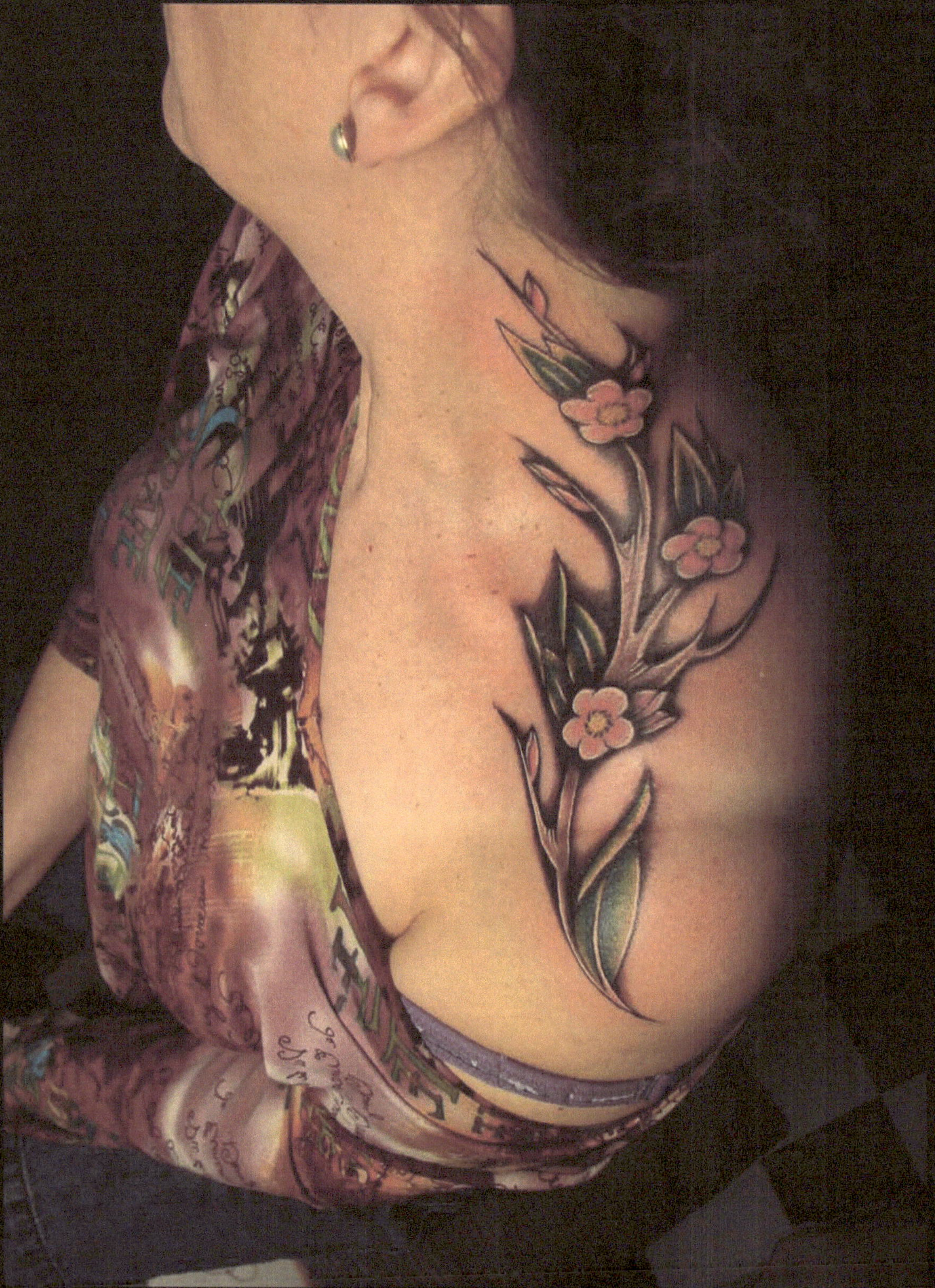

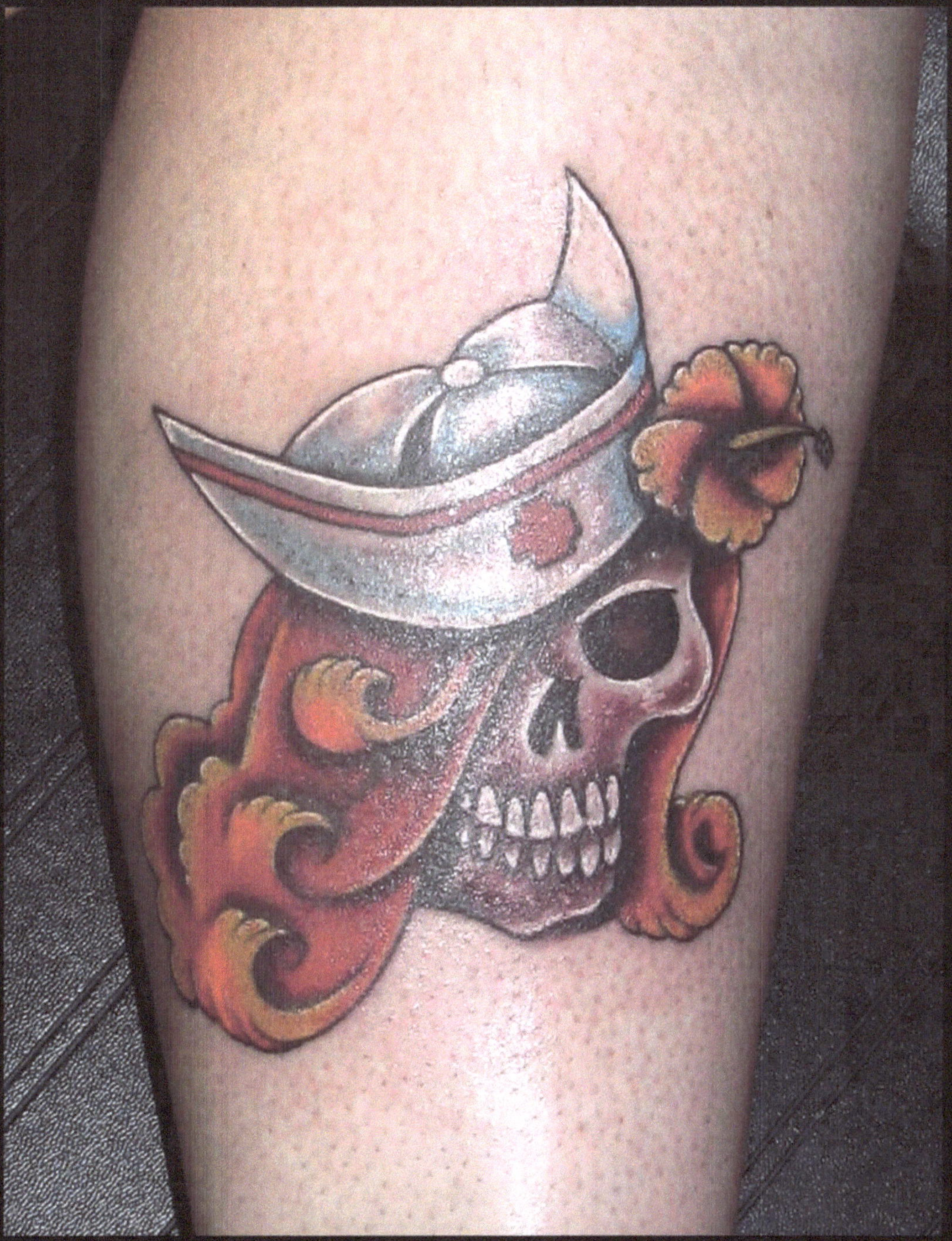

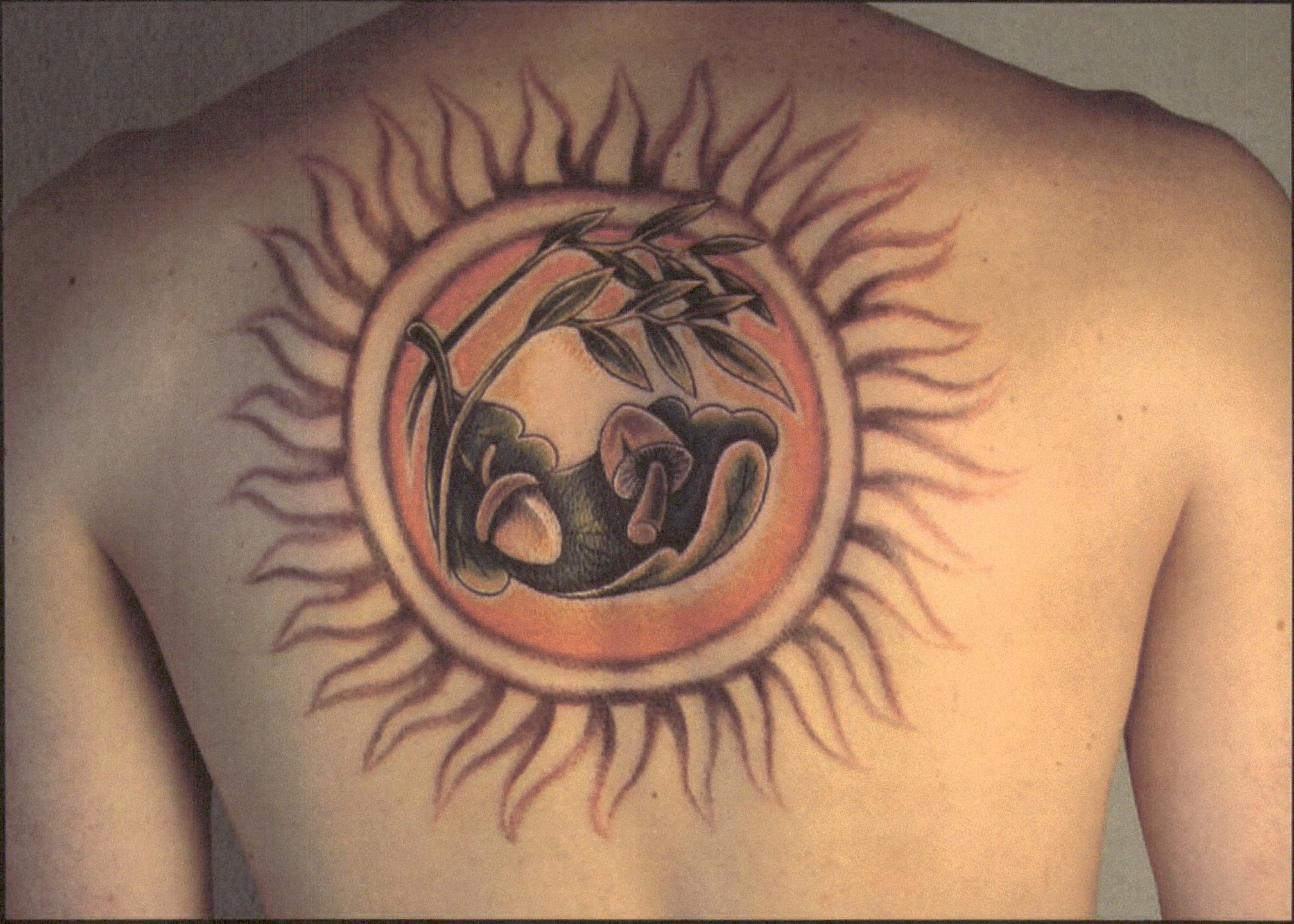

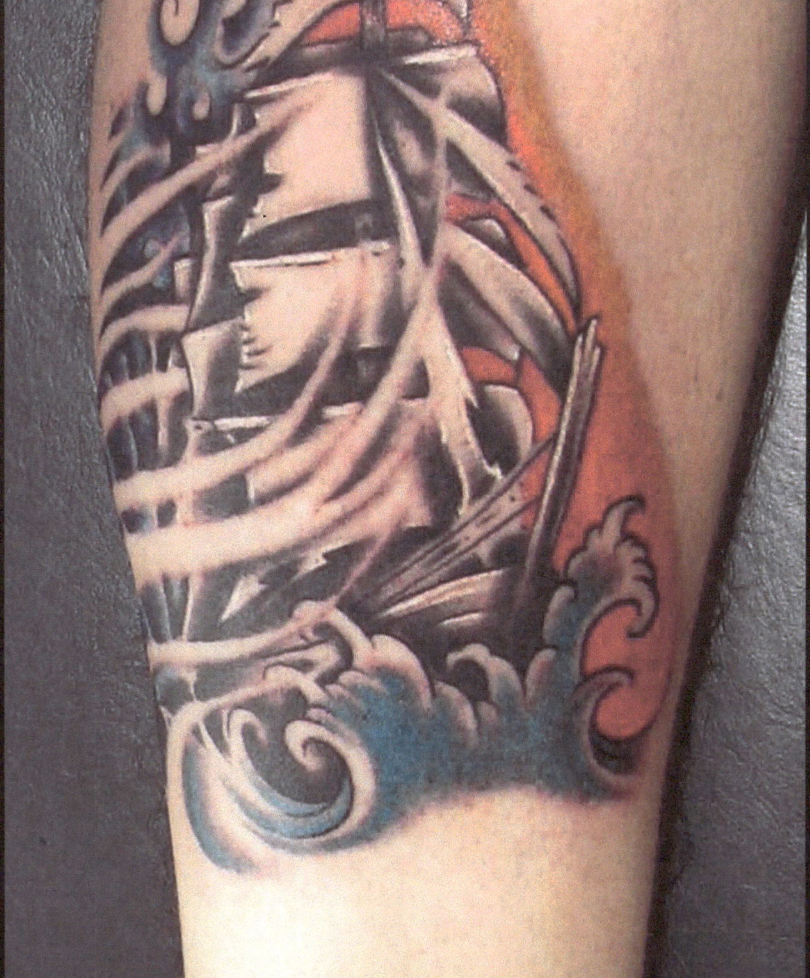

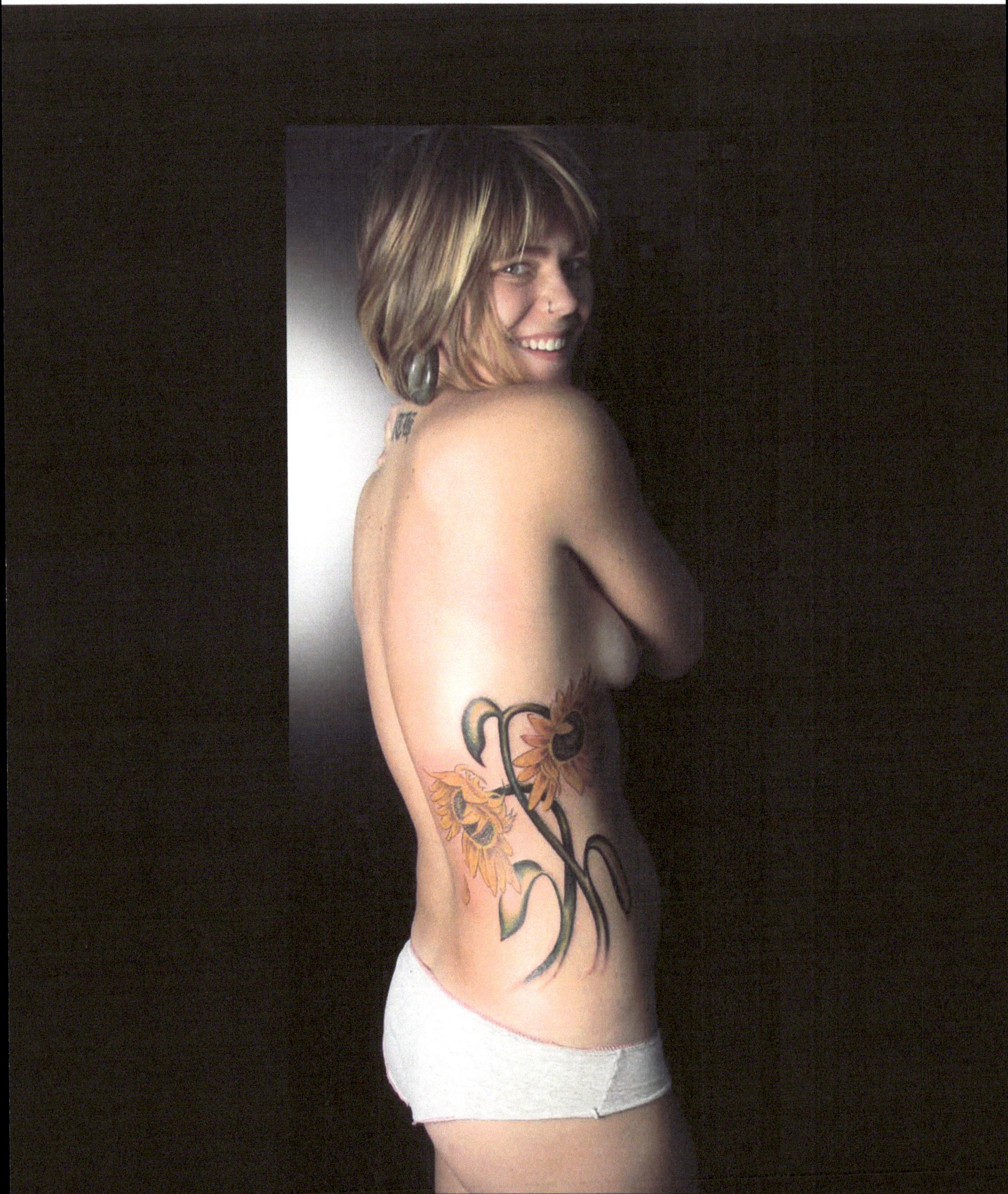

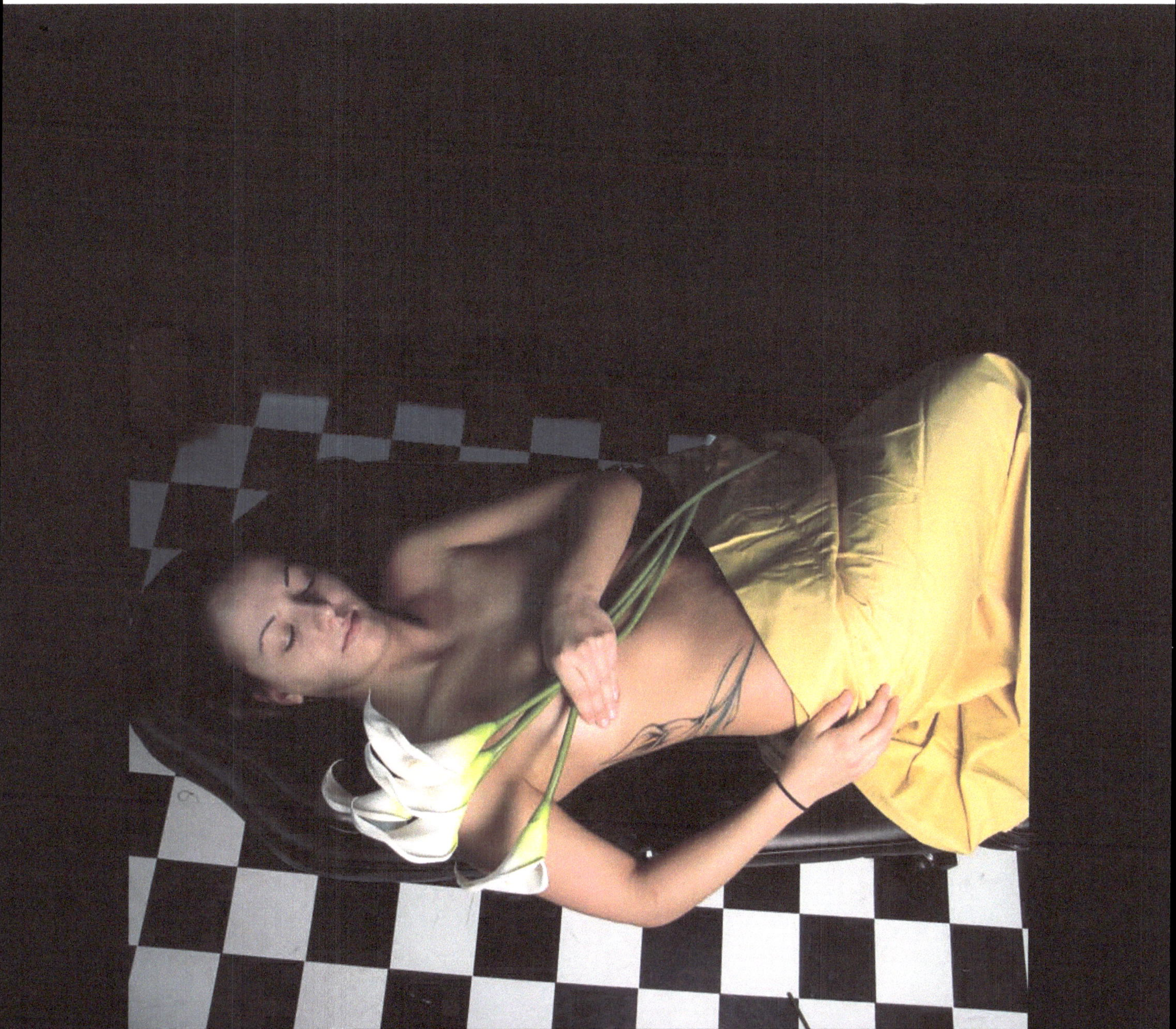

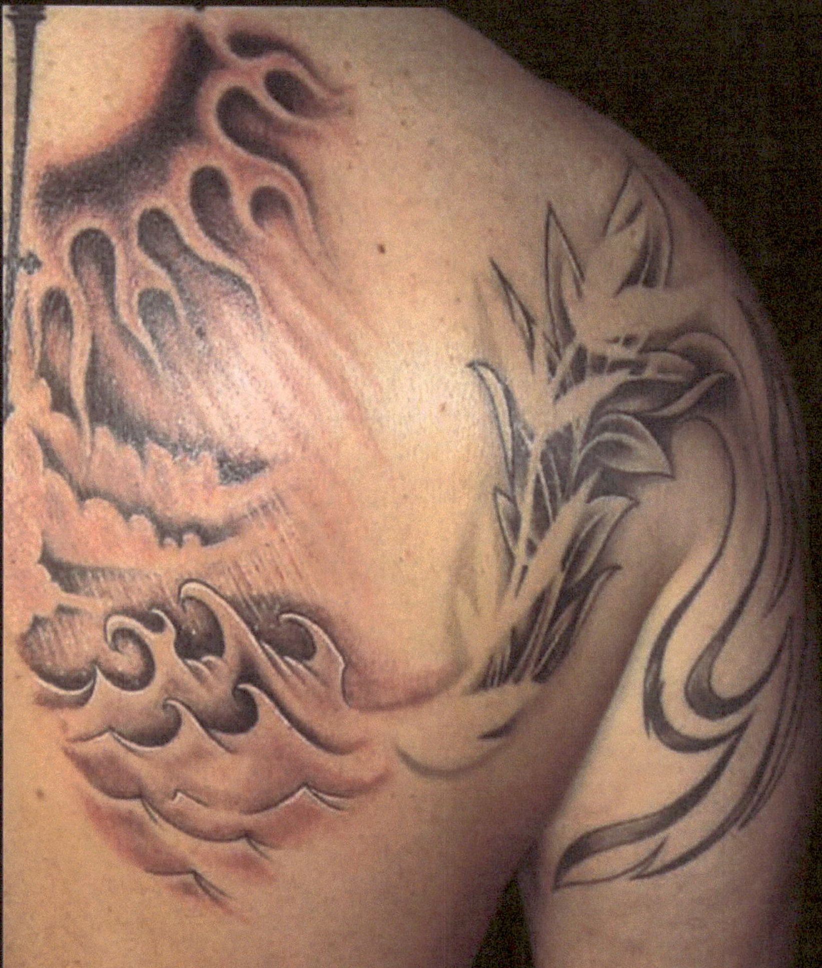

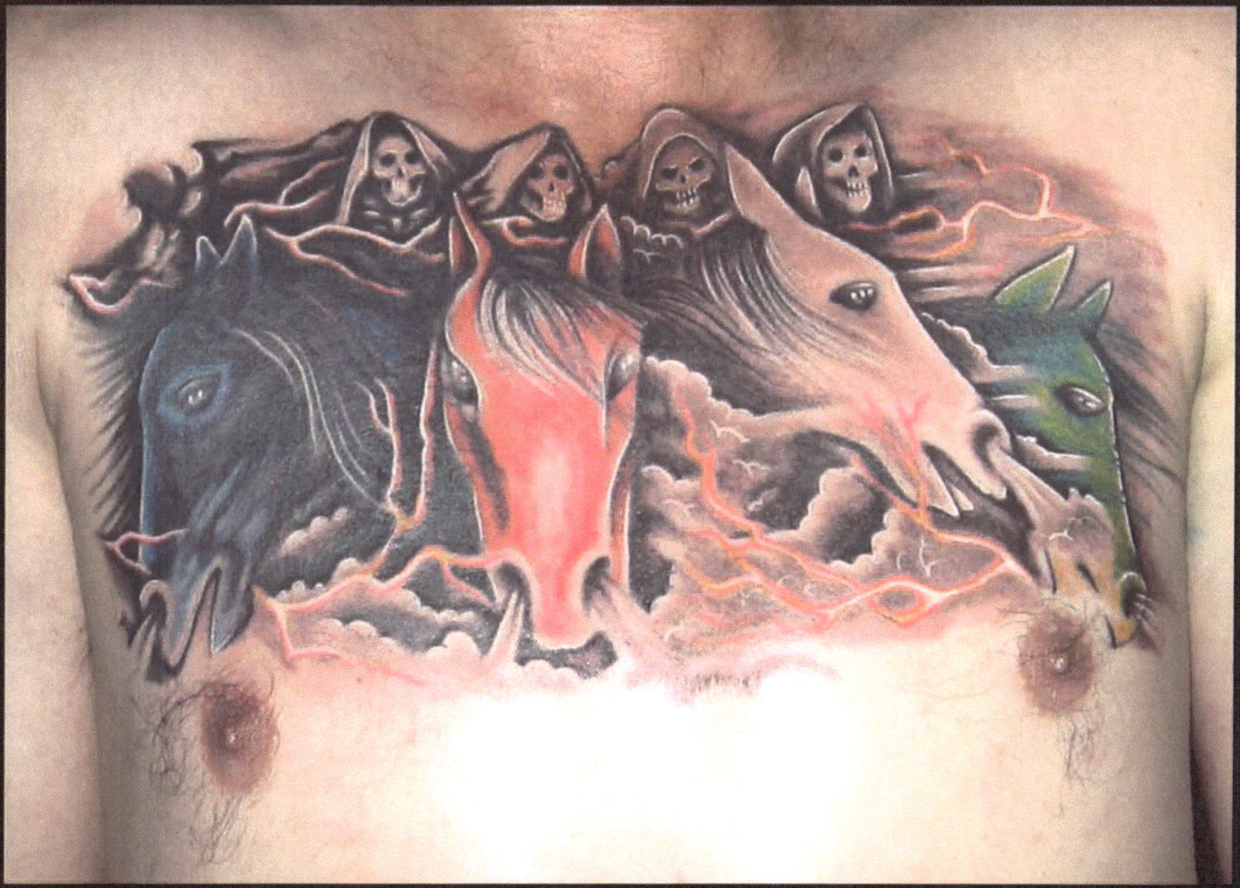

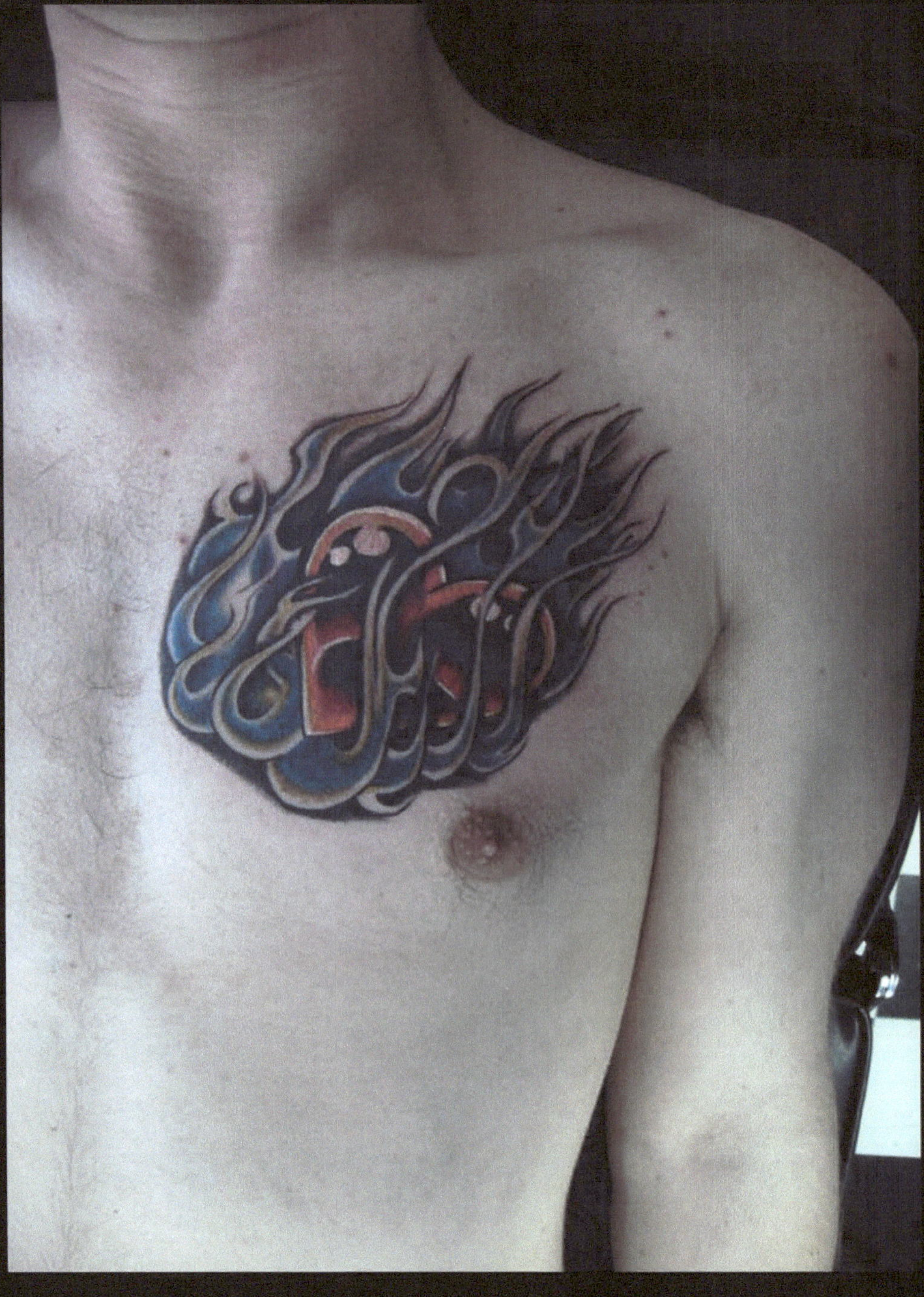

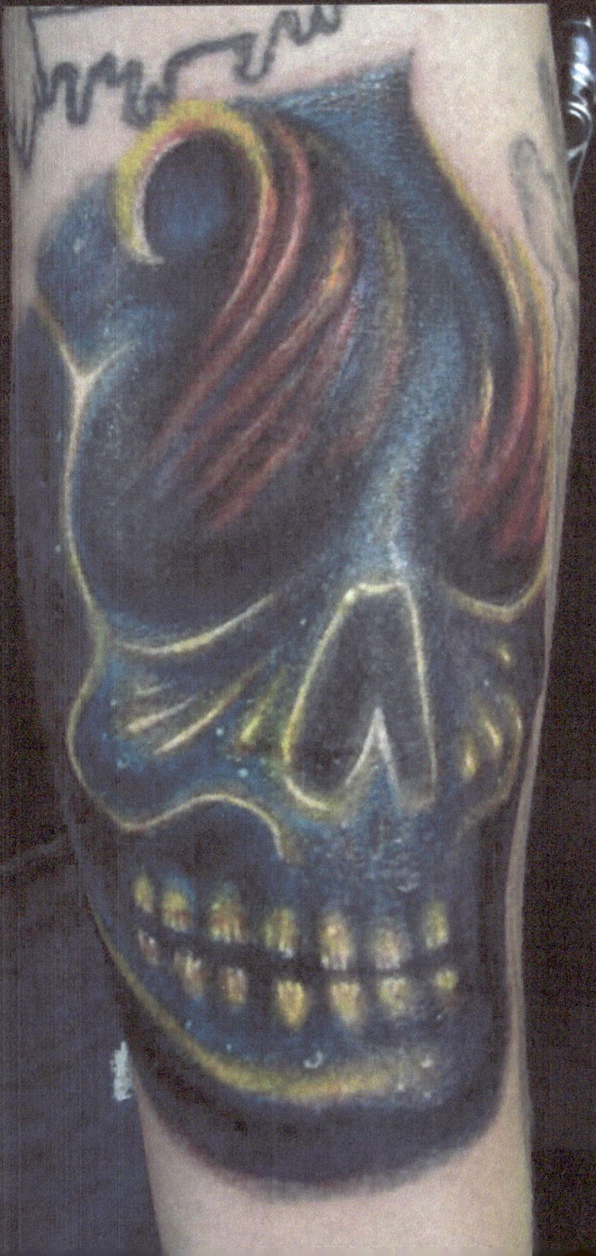

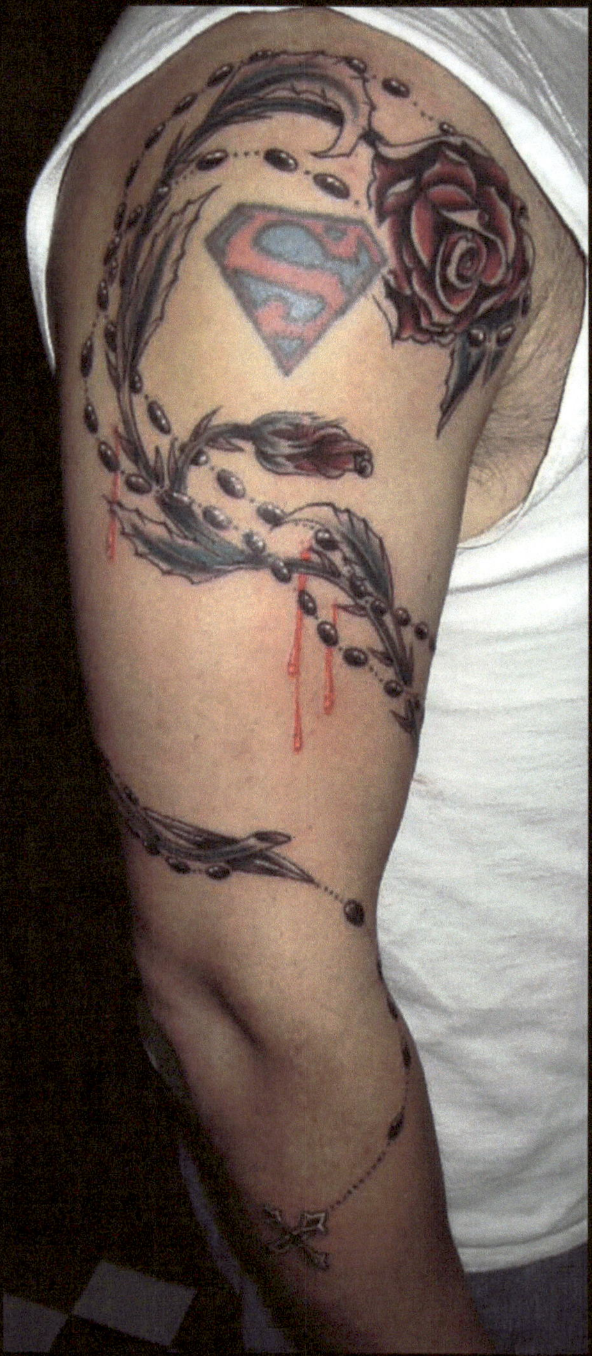

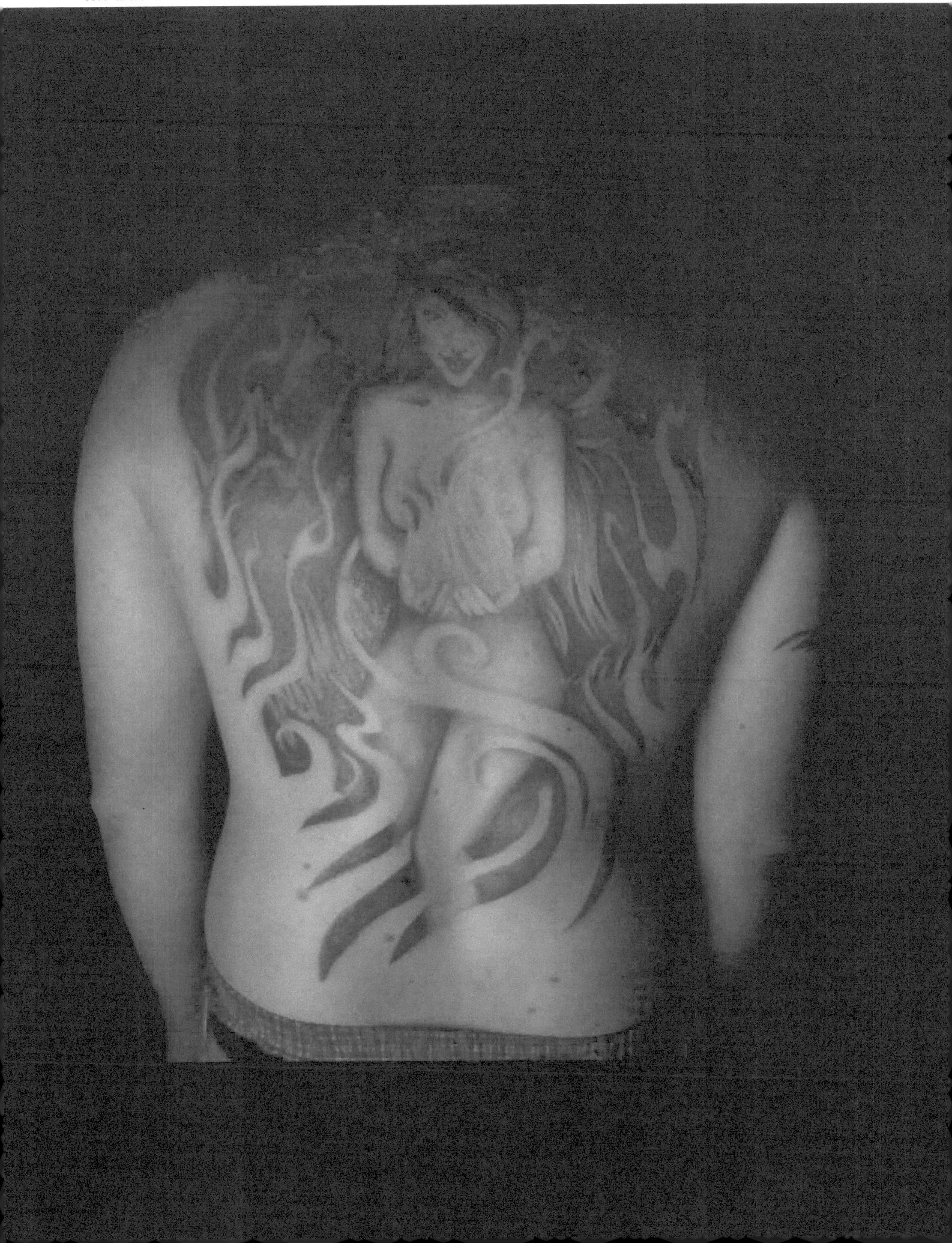

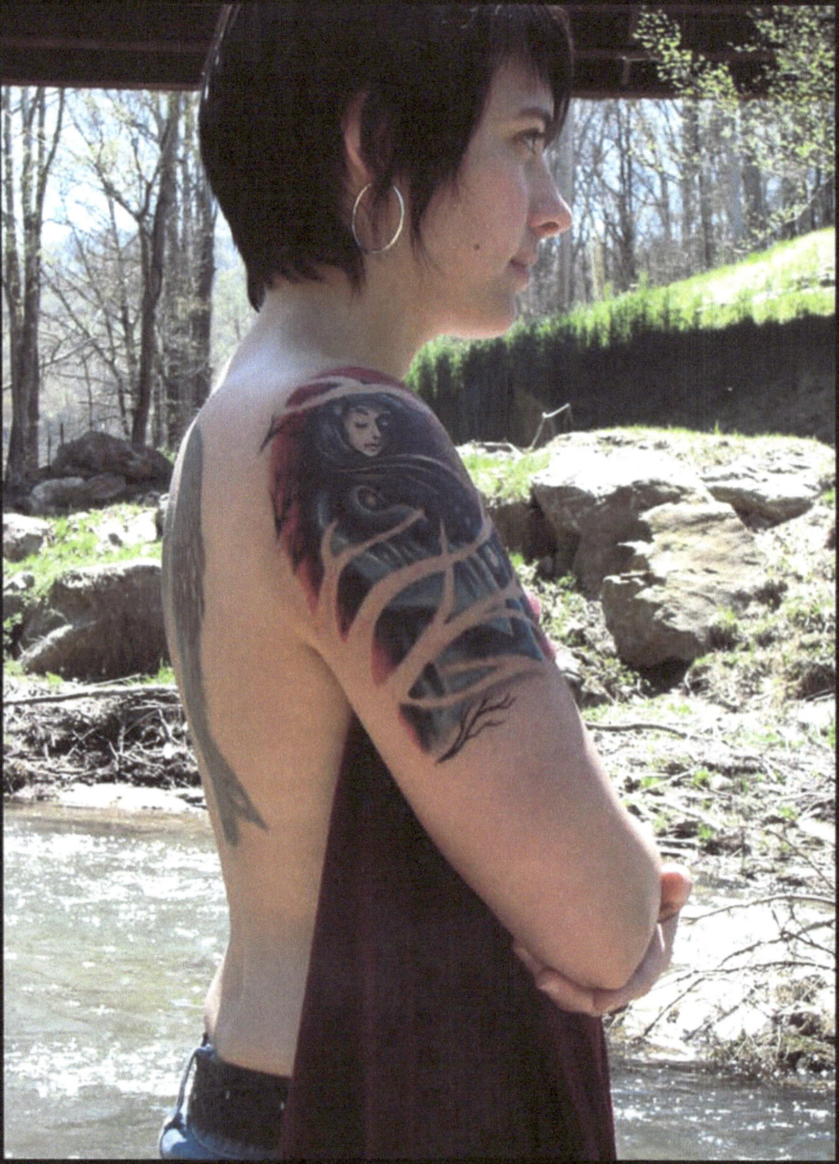

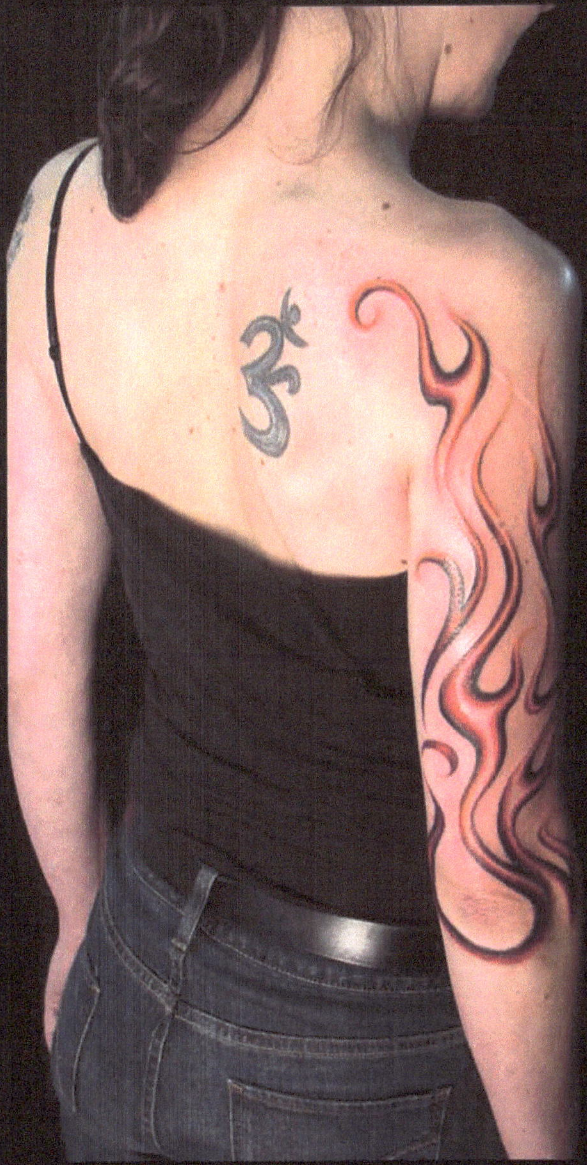

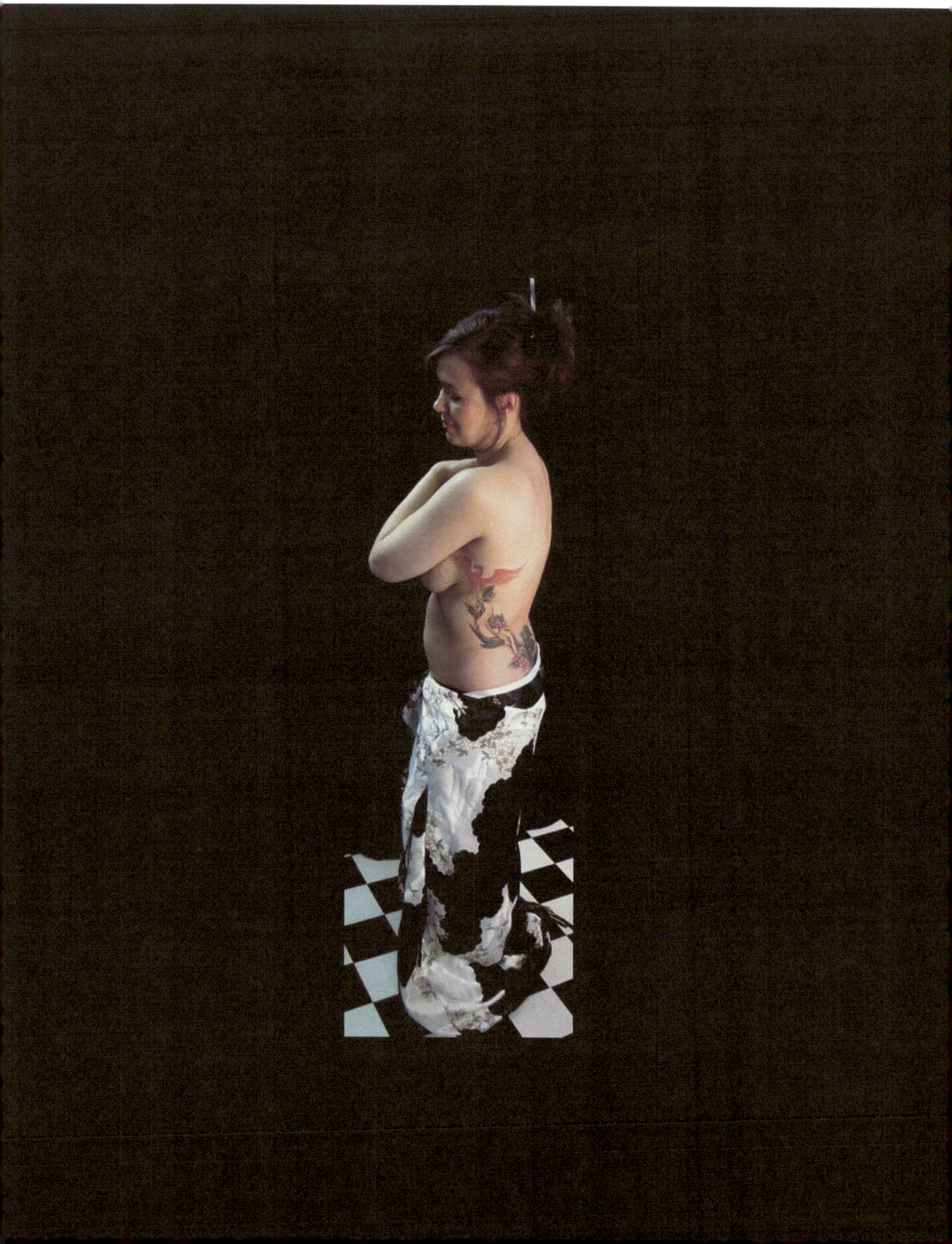

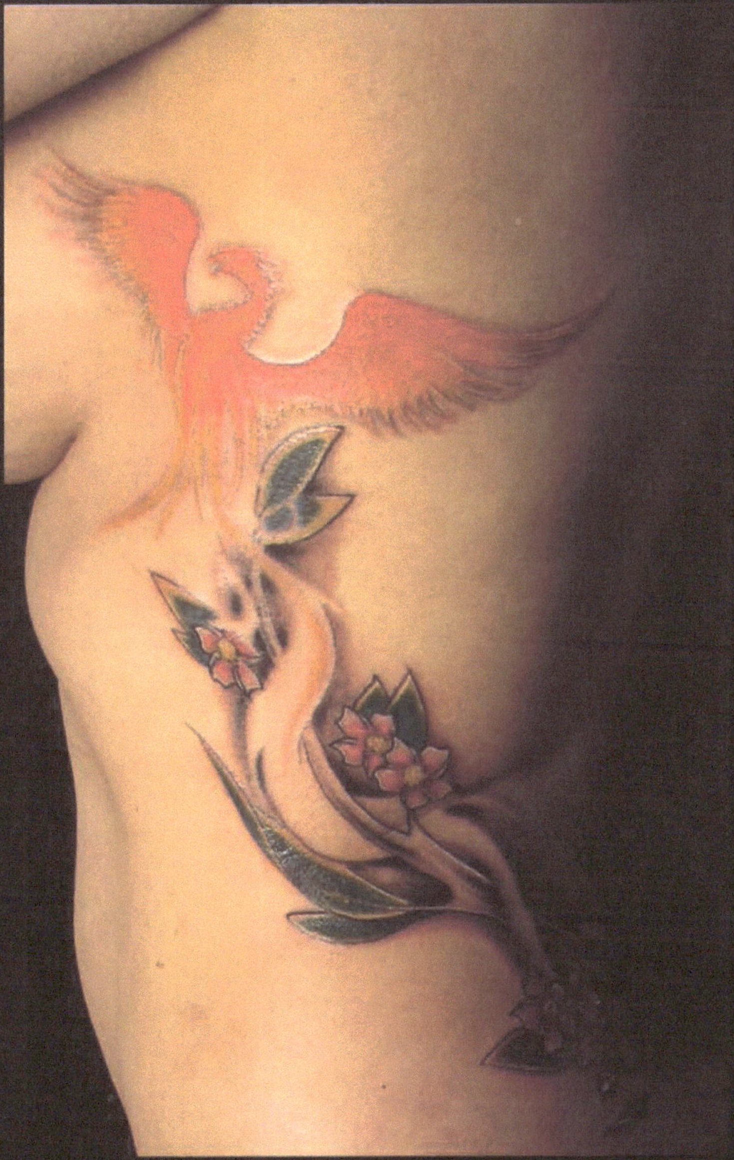

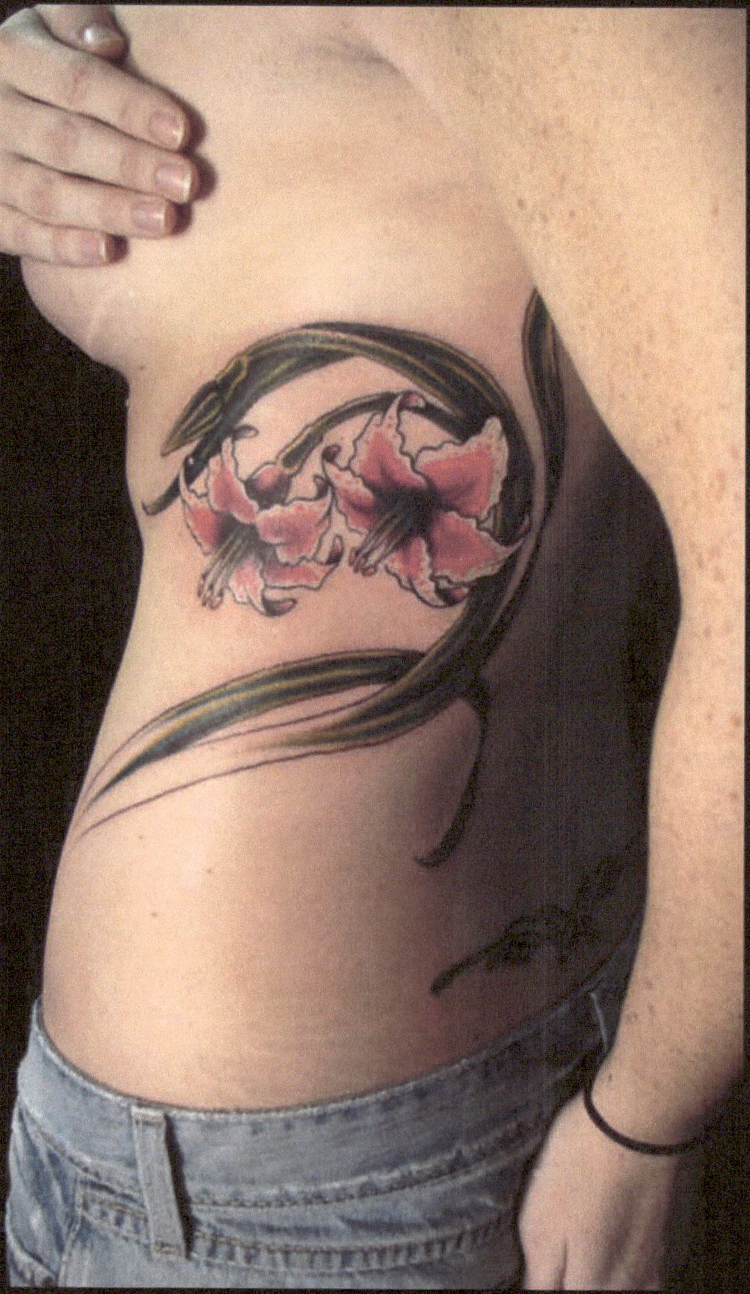

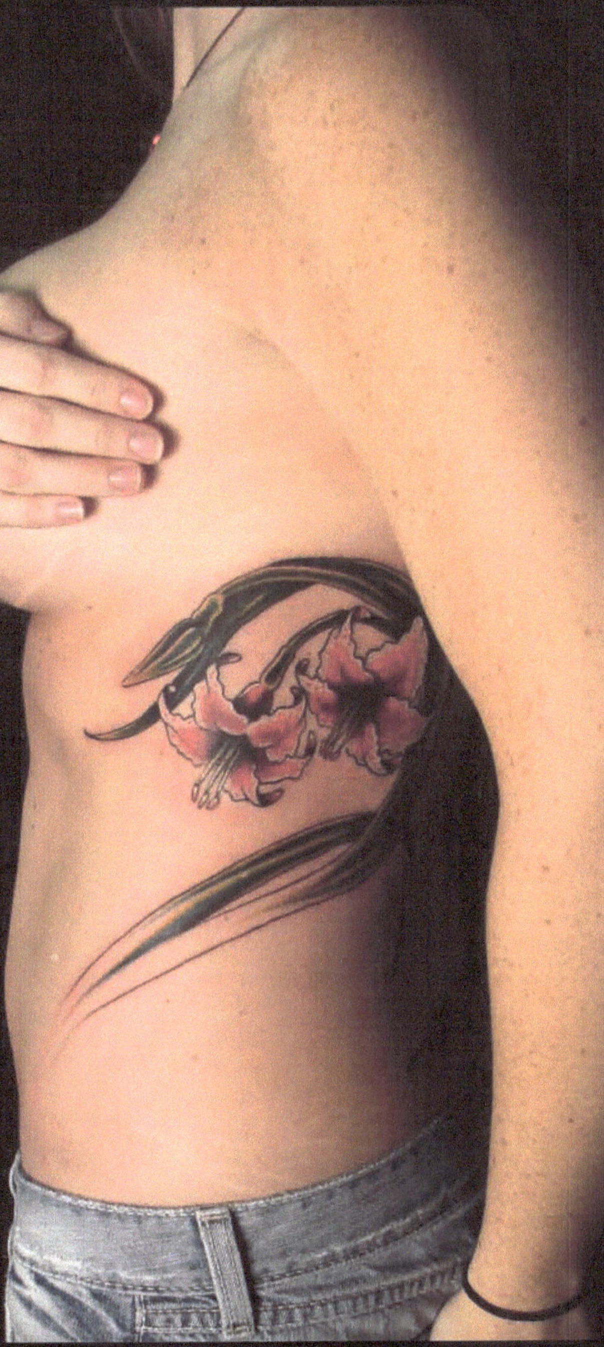

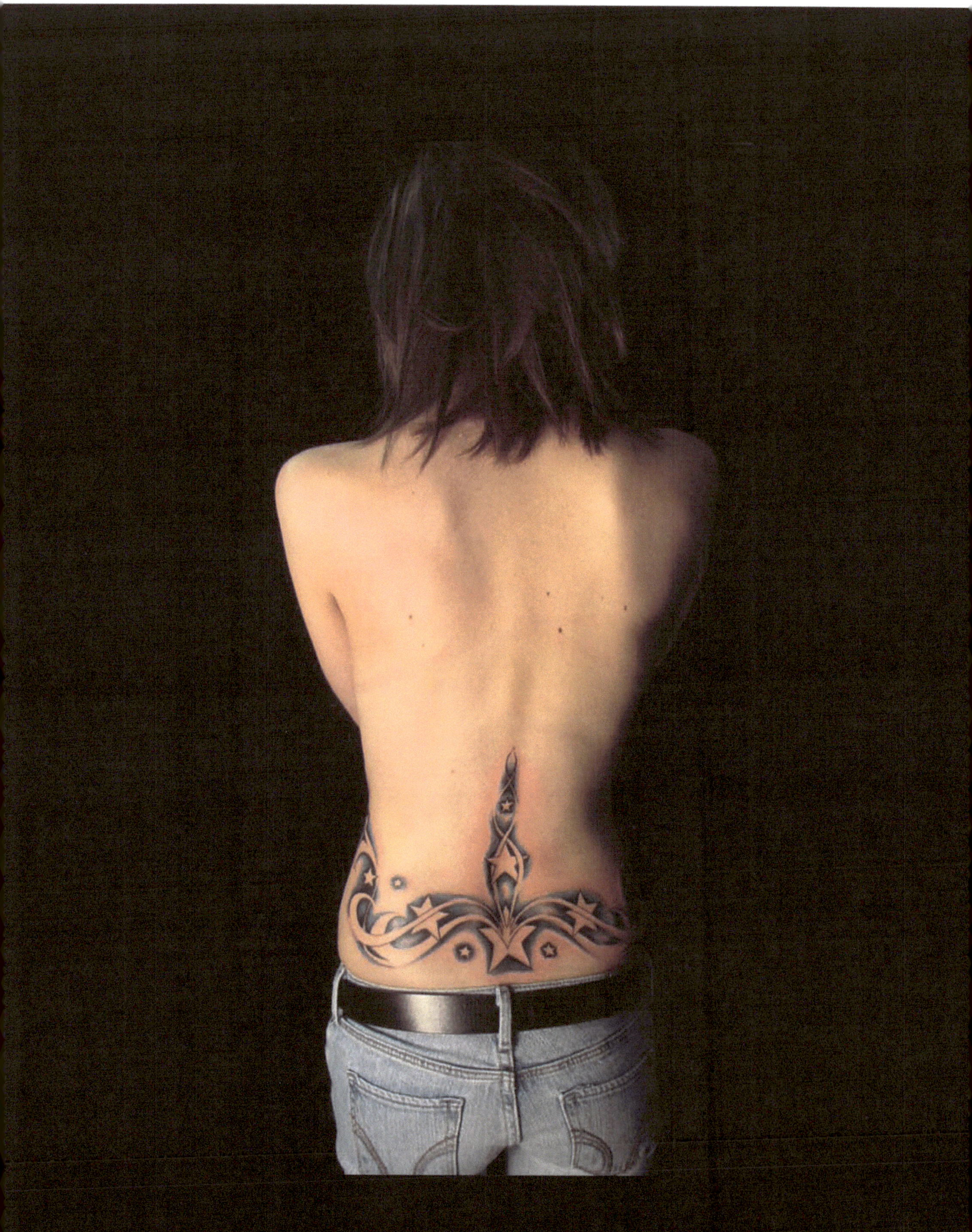

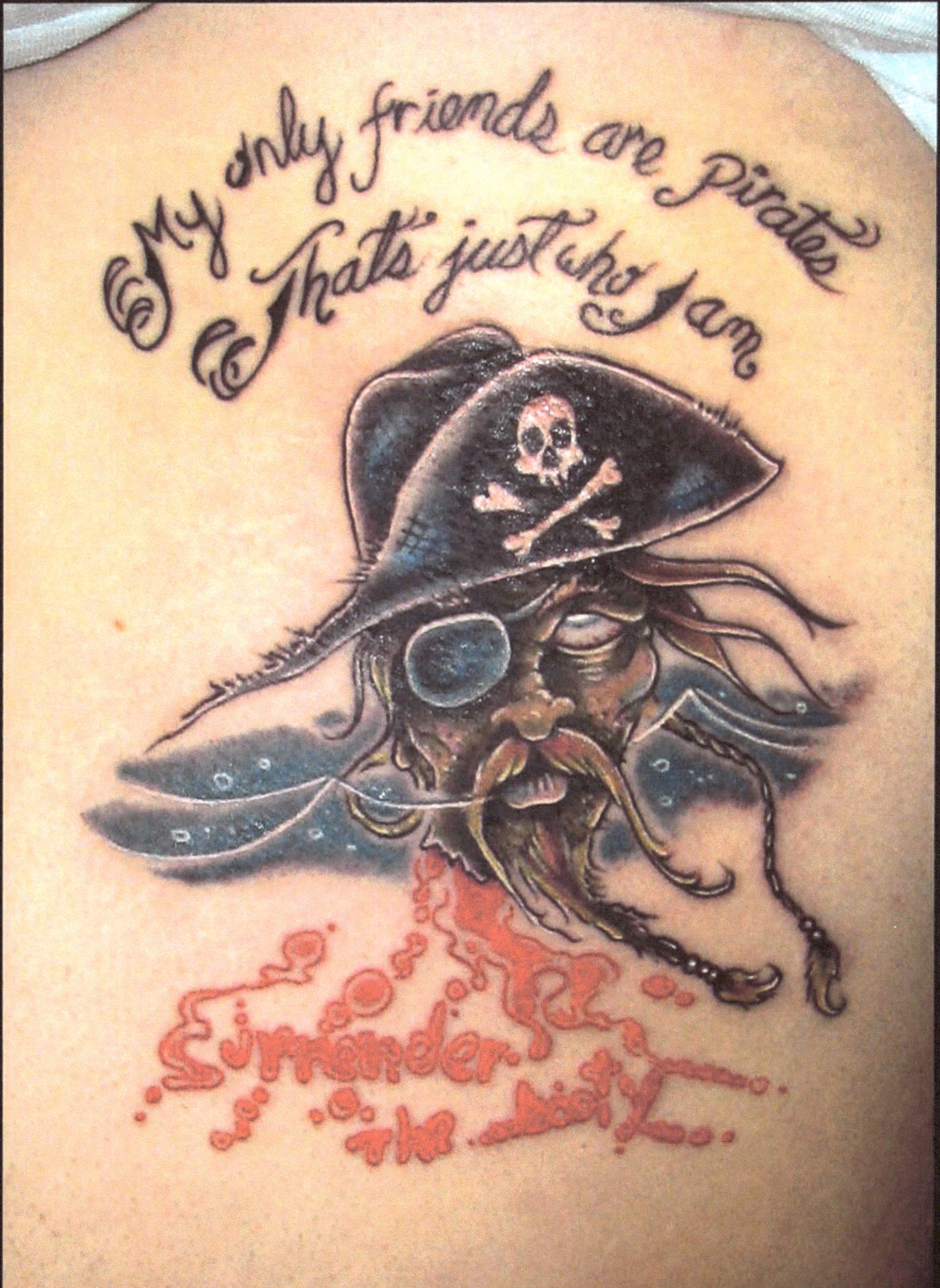
My only friends are pirates
That's just who I am
Surrender
the booty...

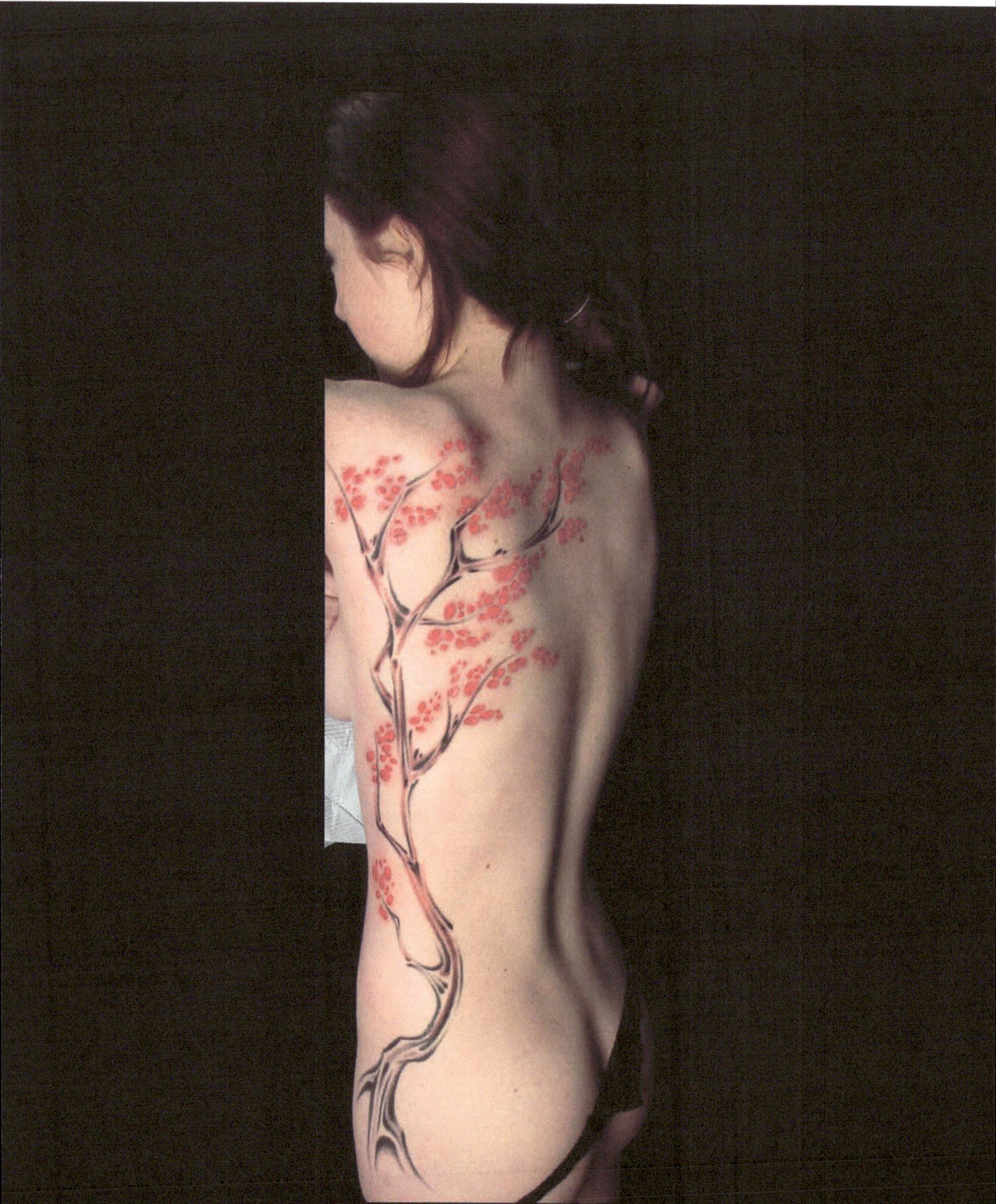

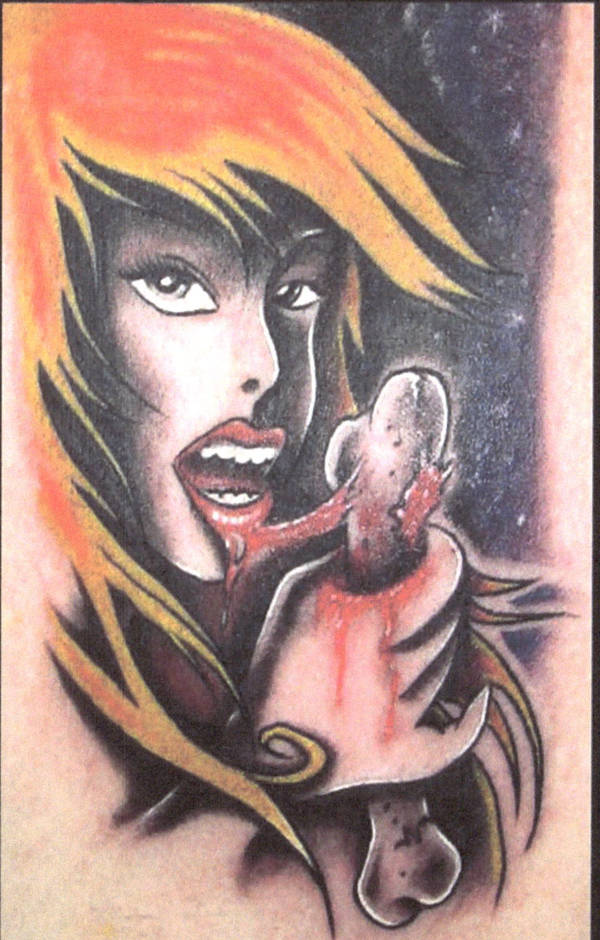

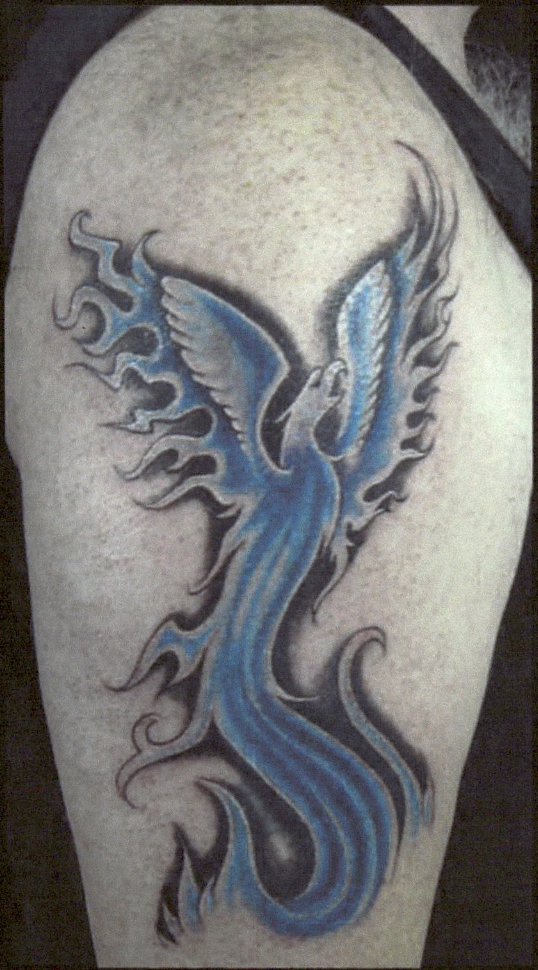

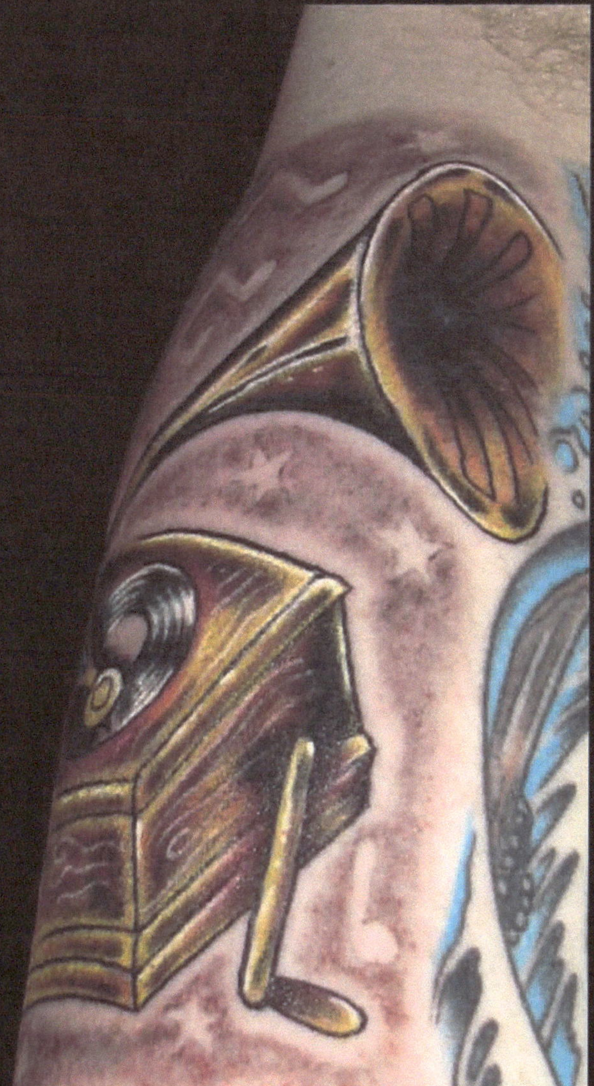

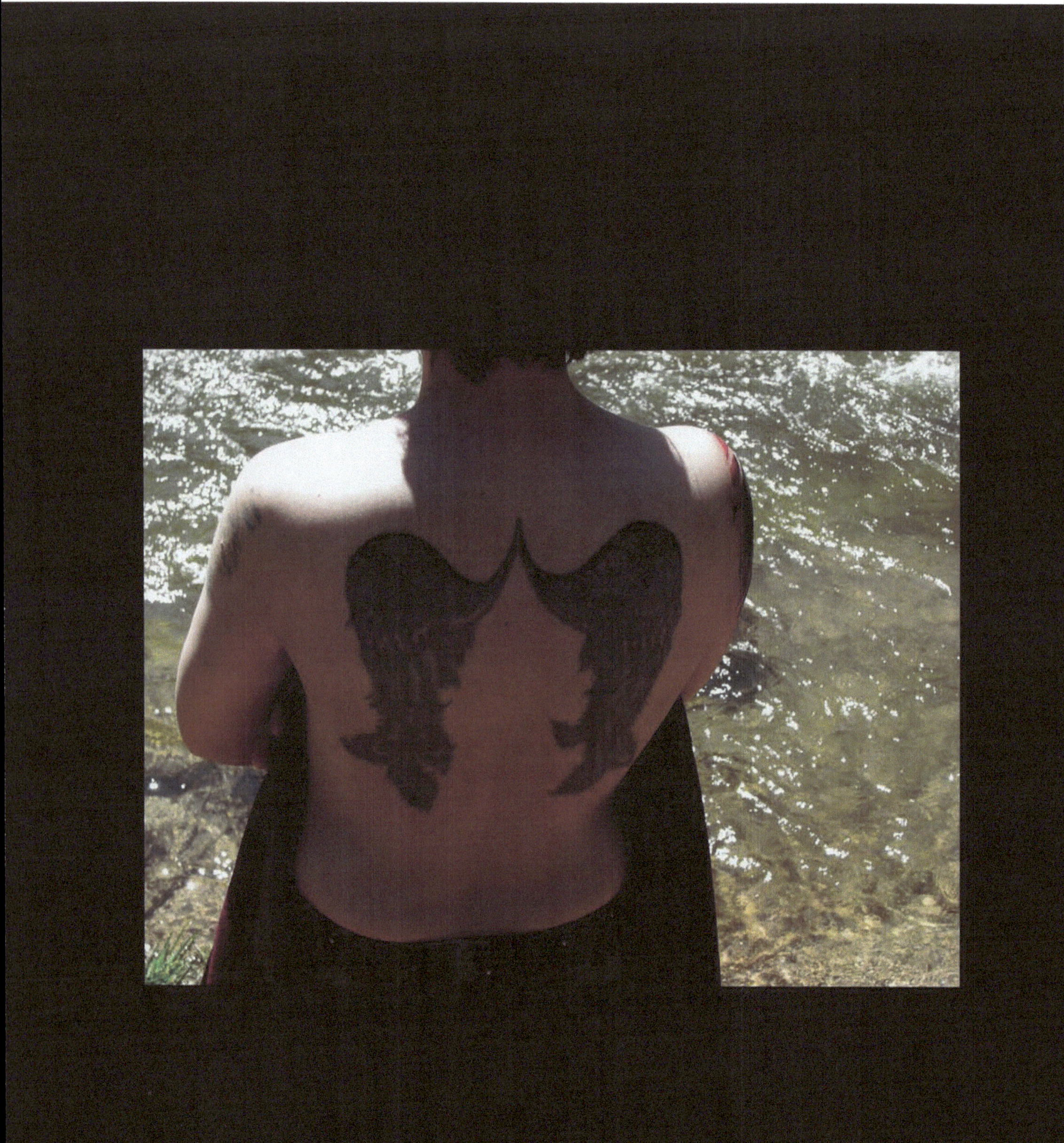

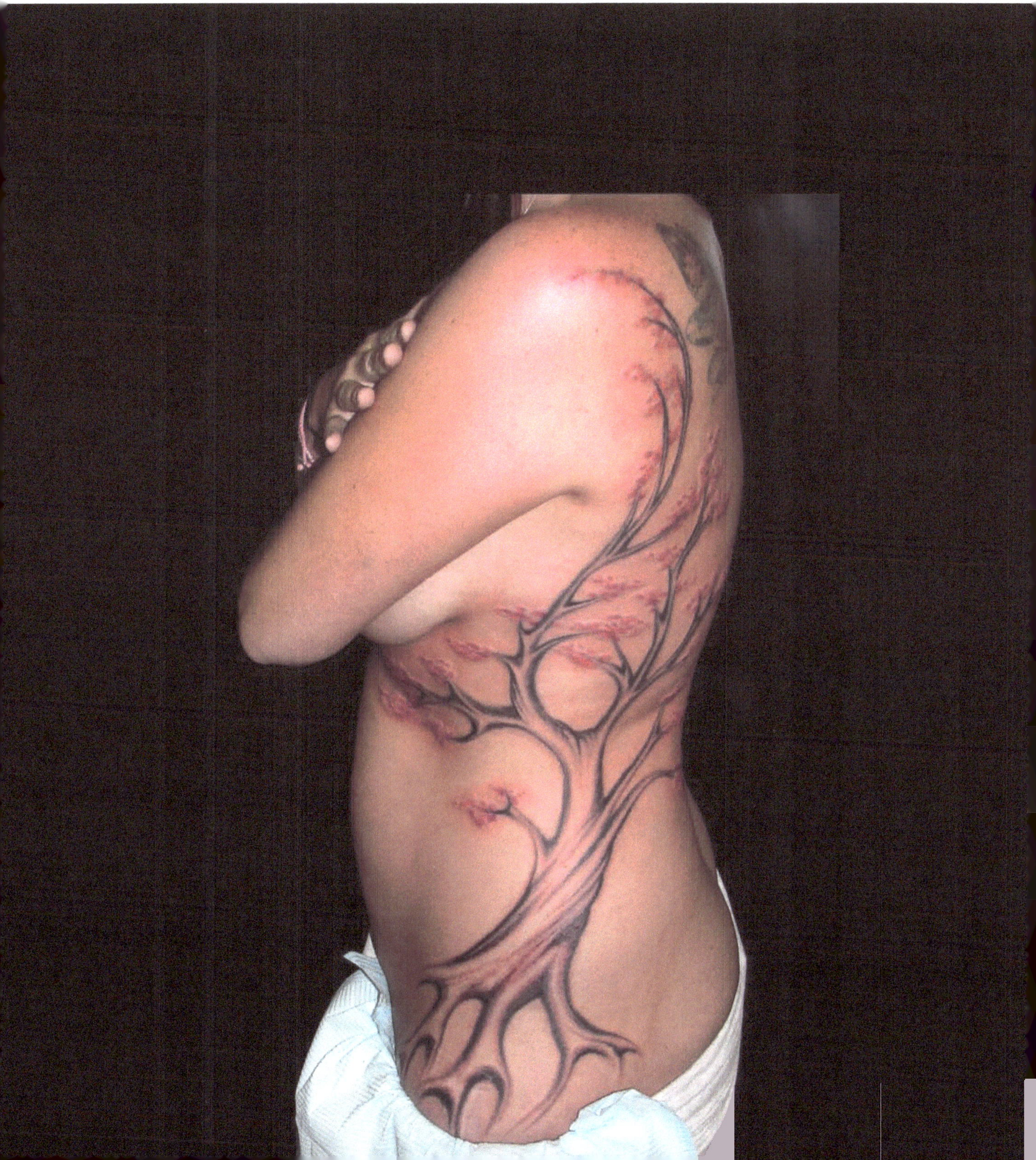

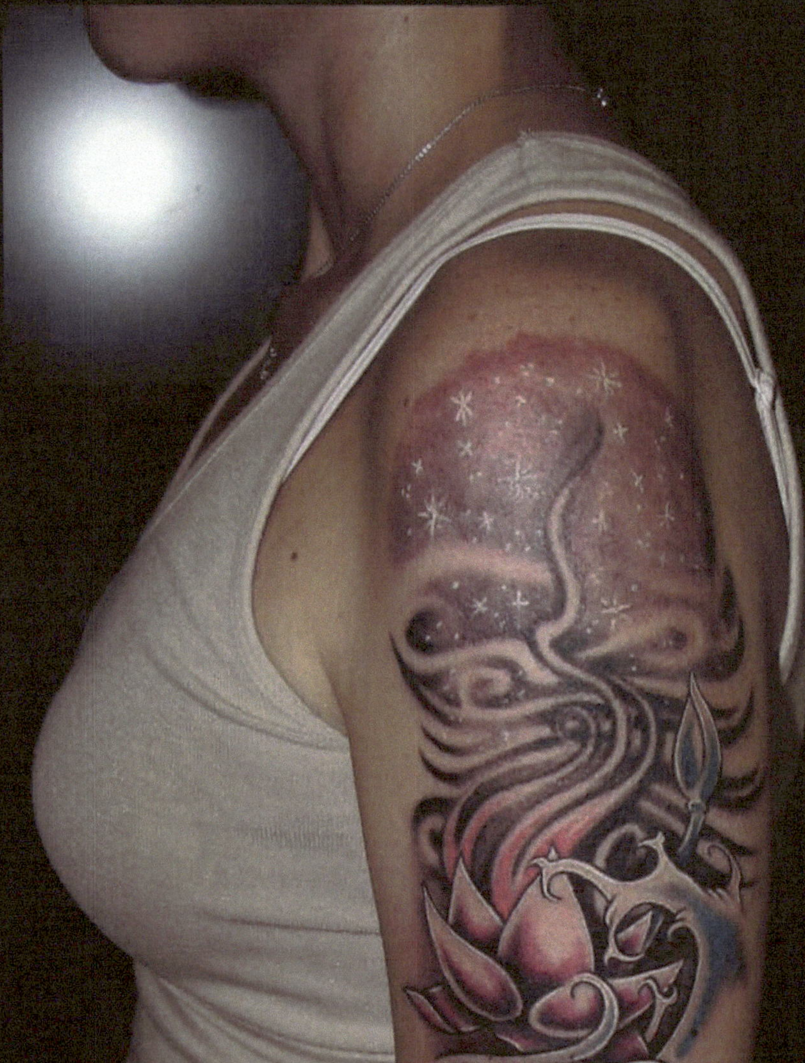

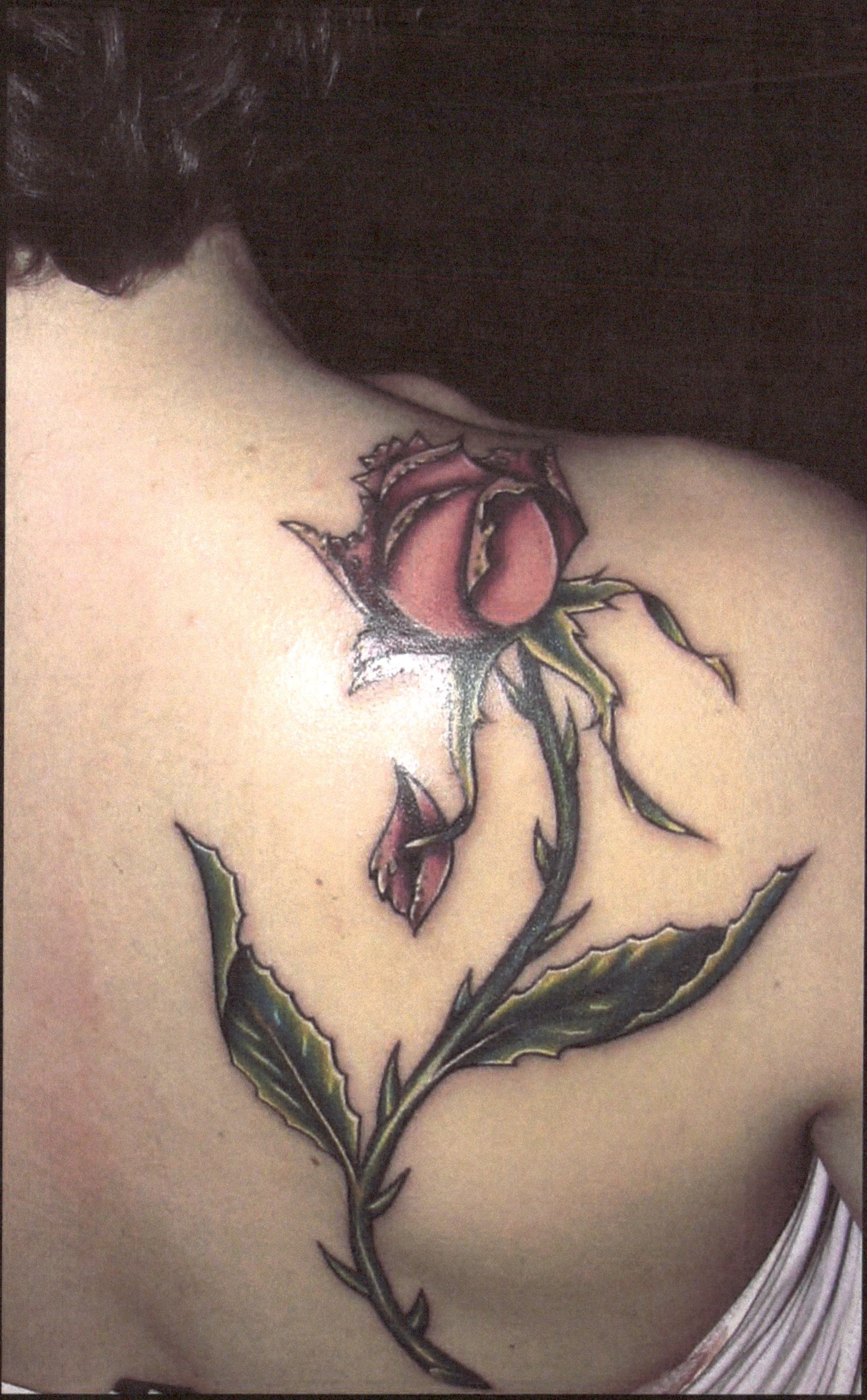

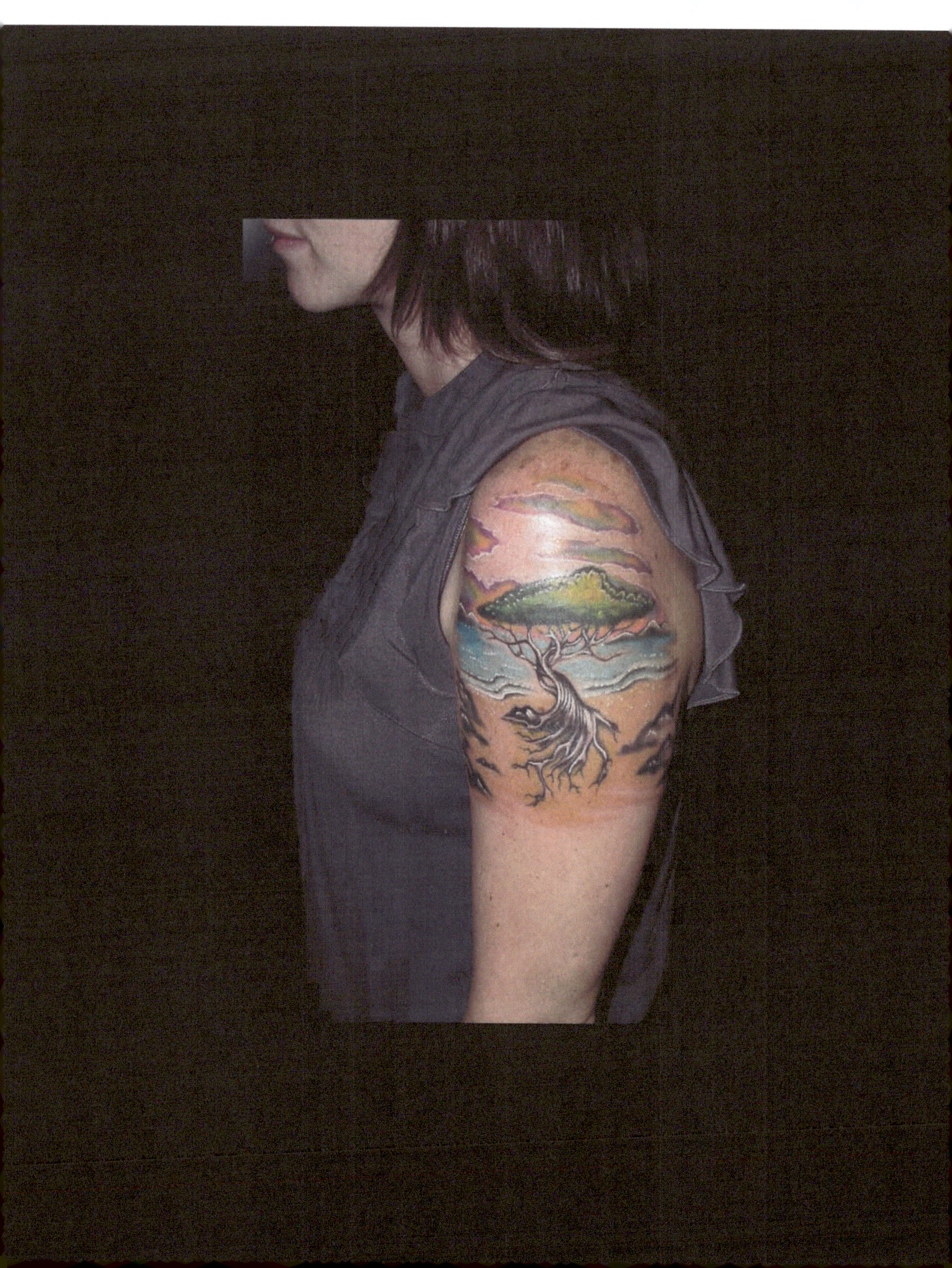

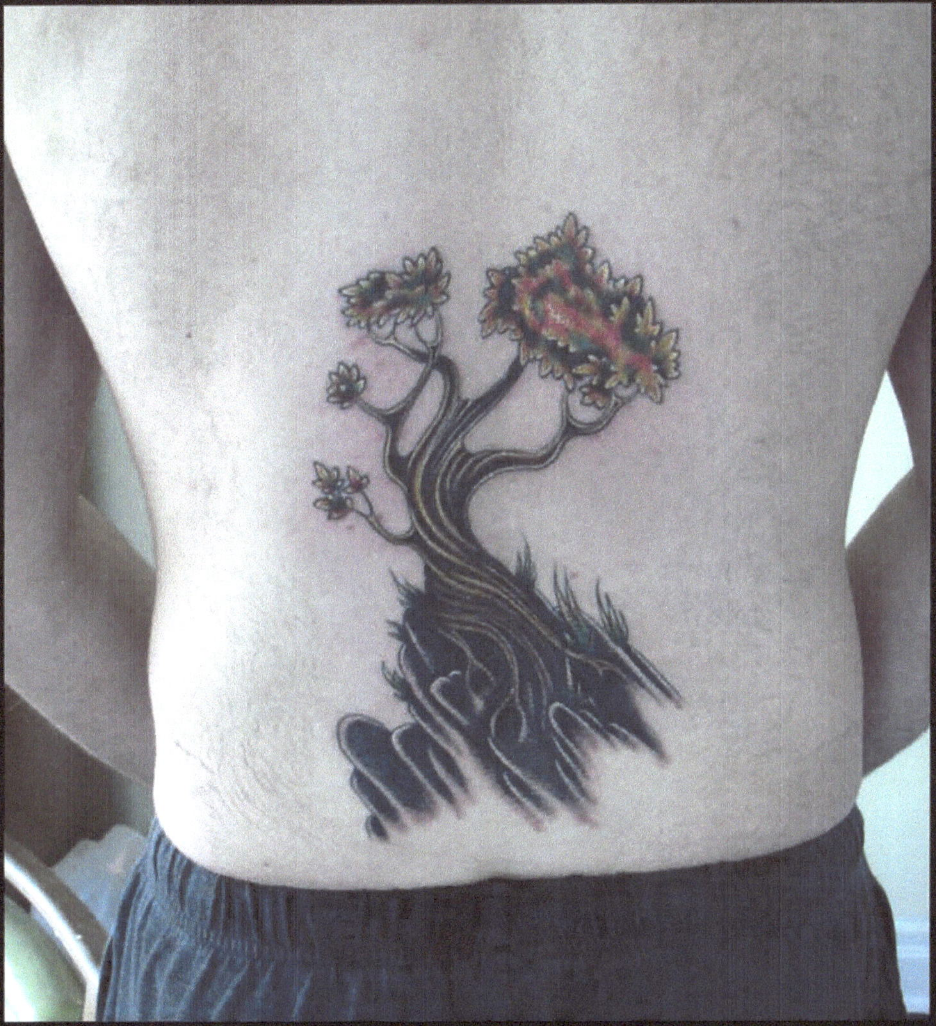

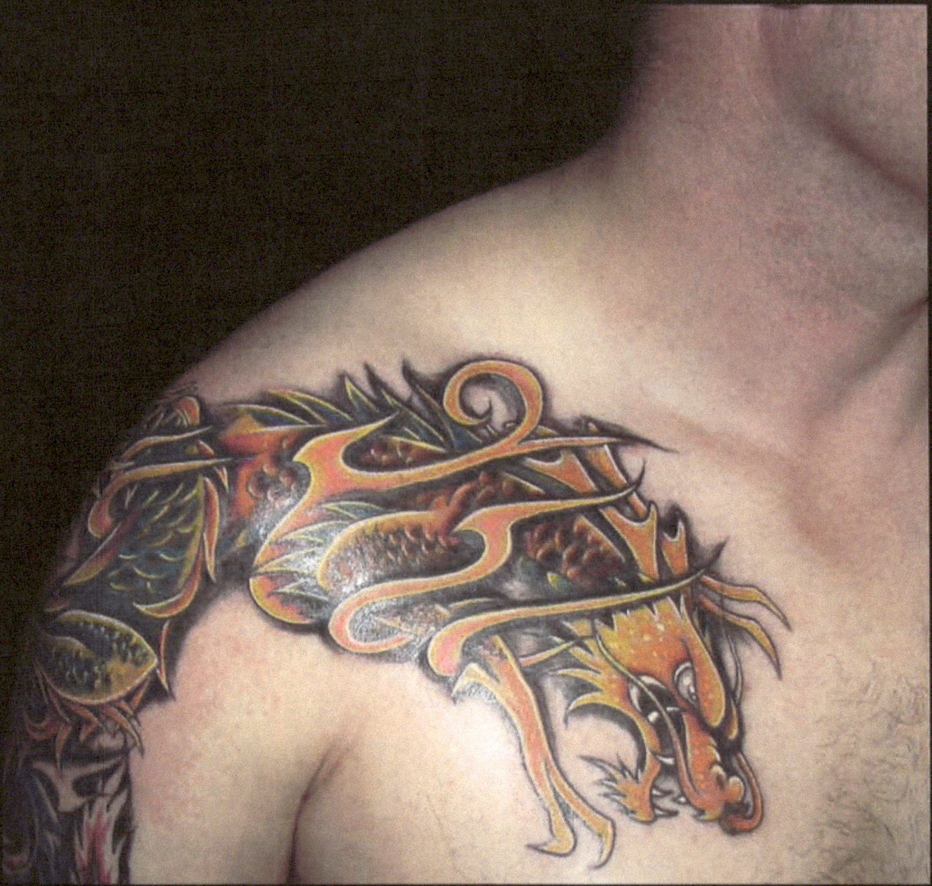
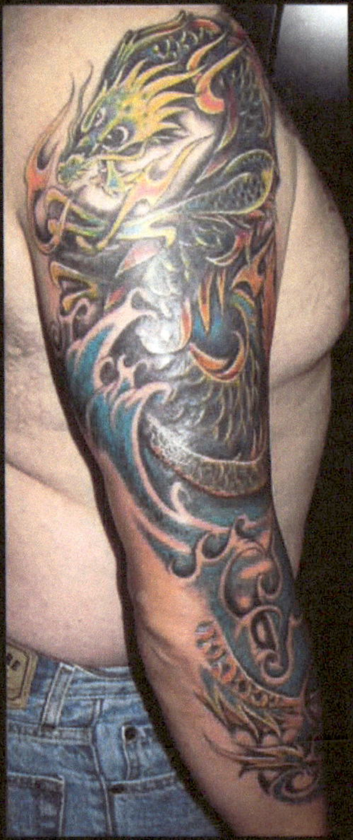
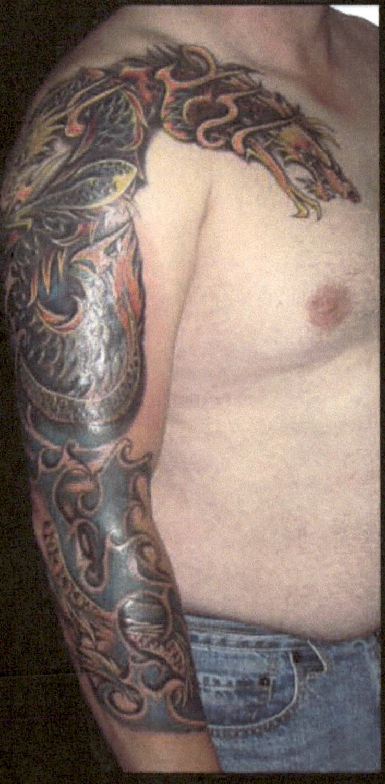

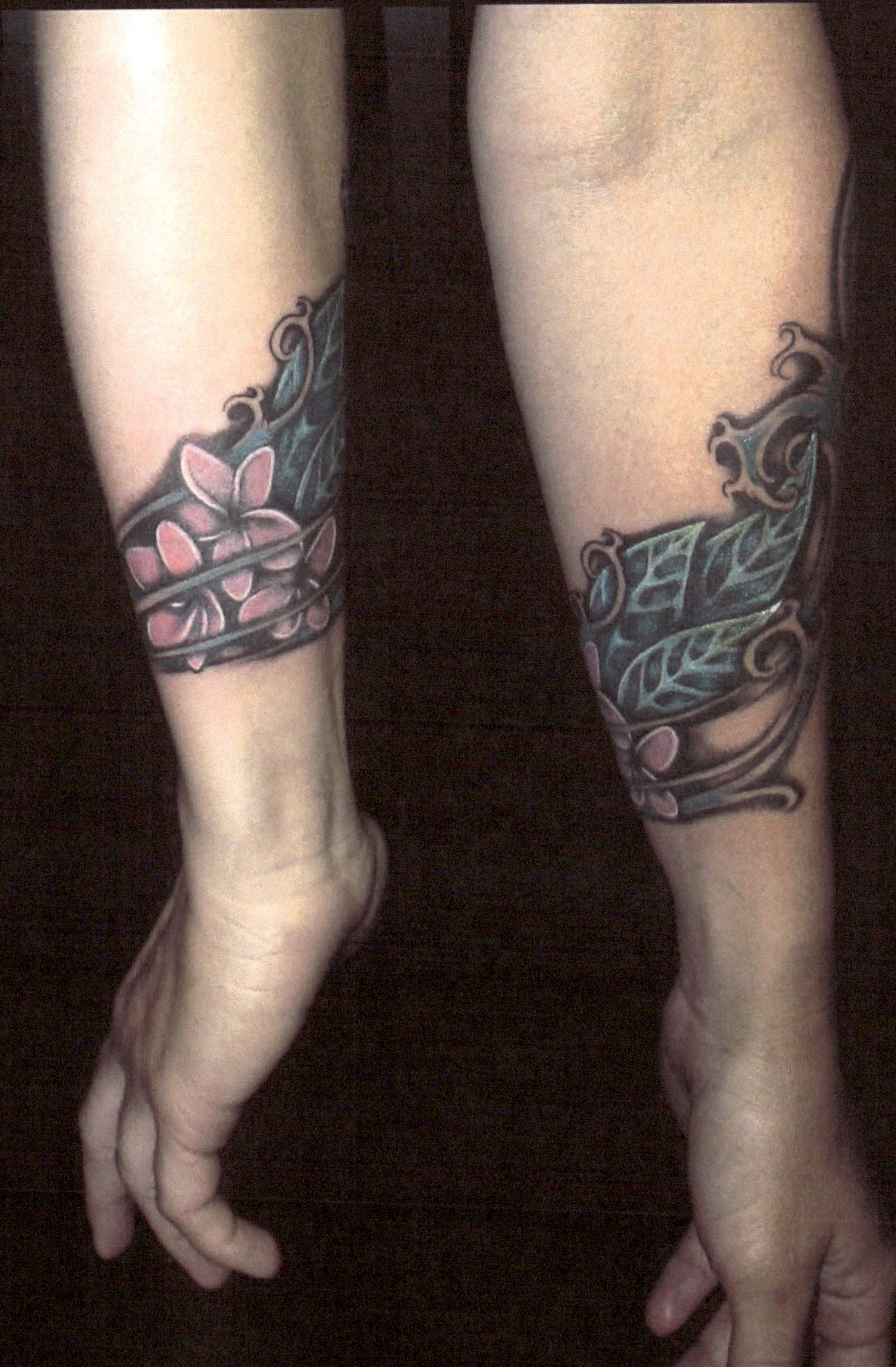

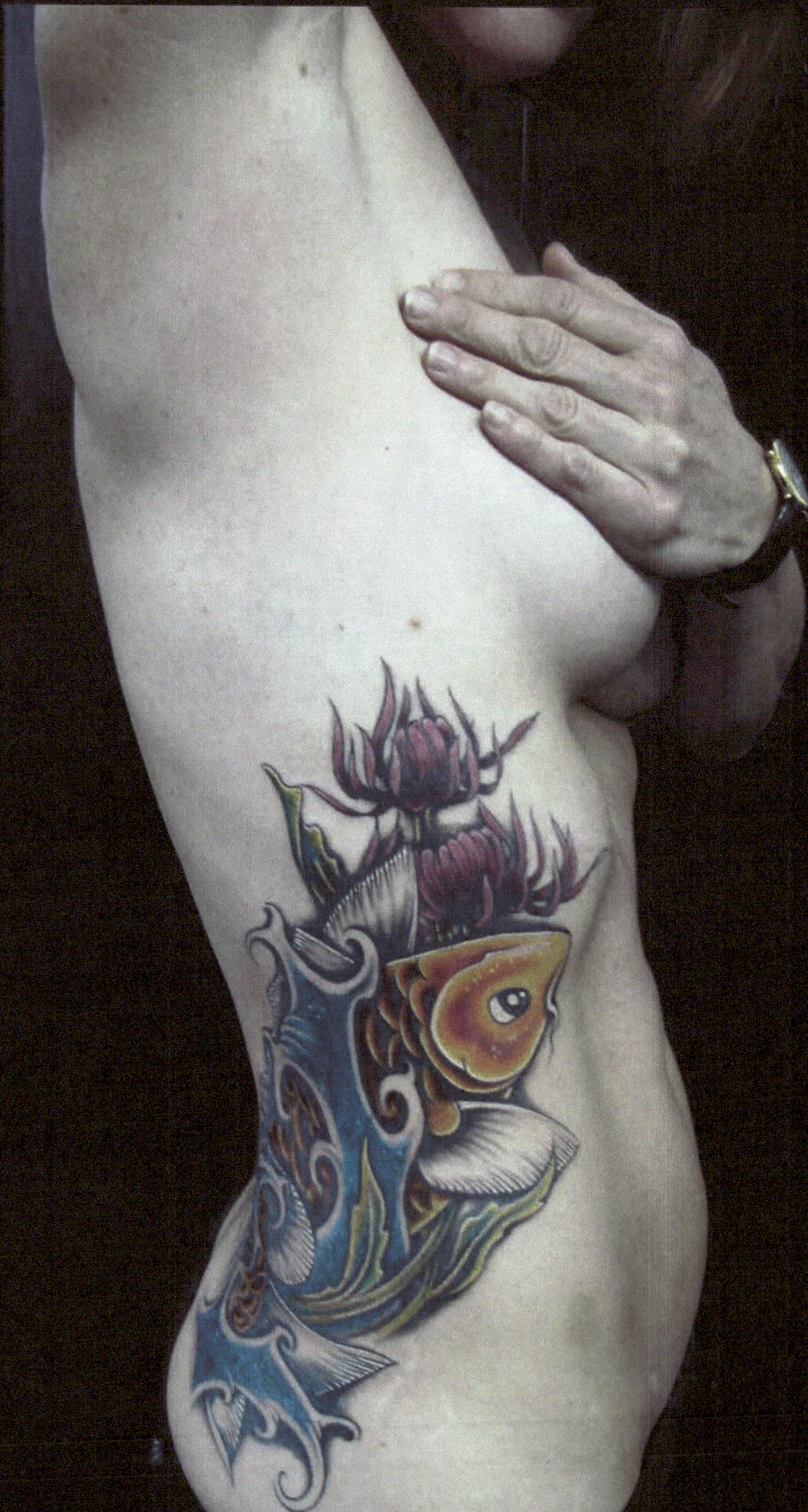

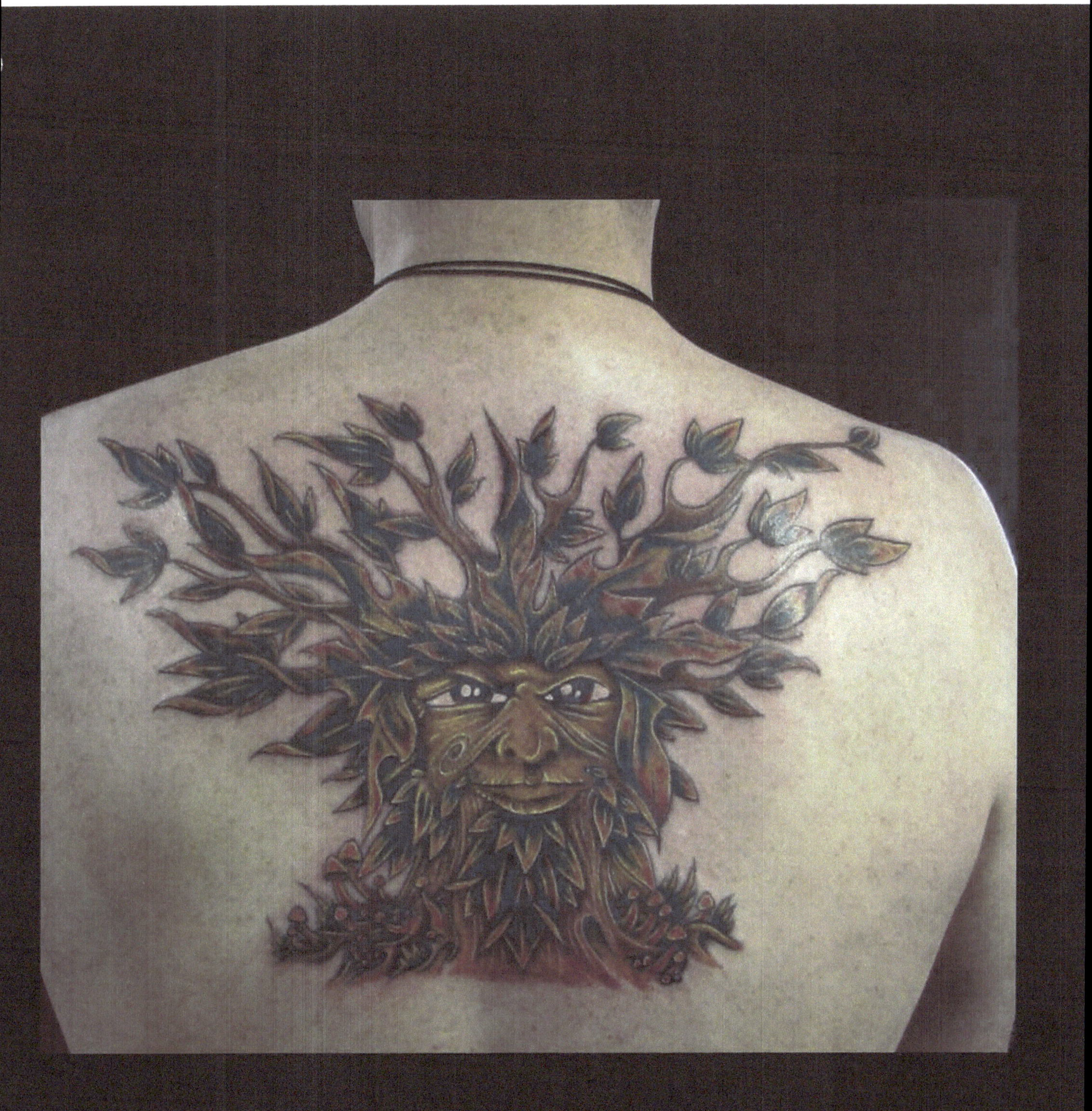

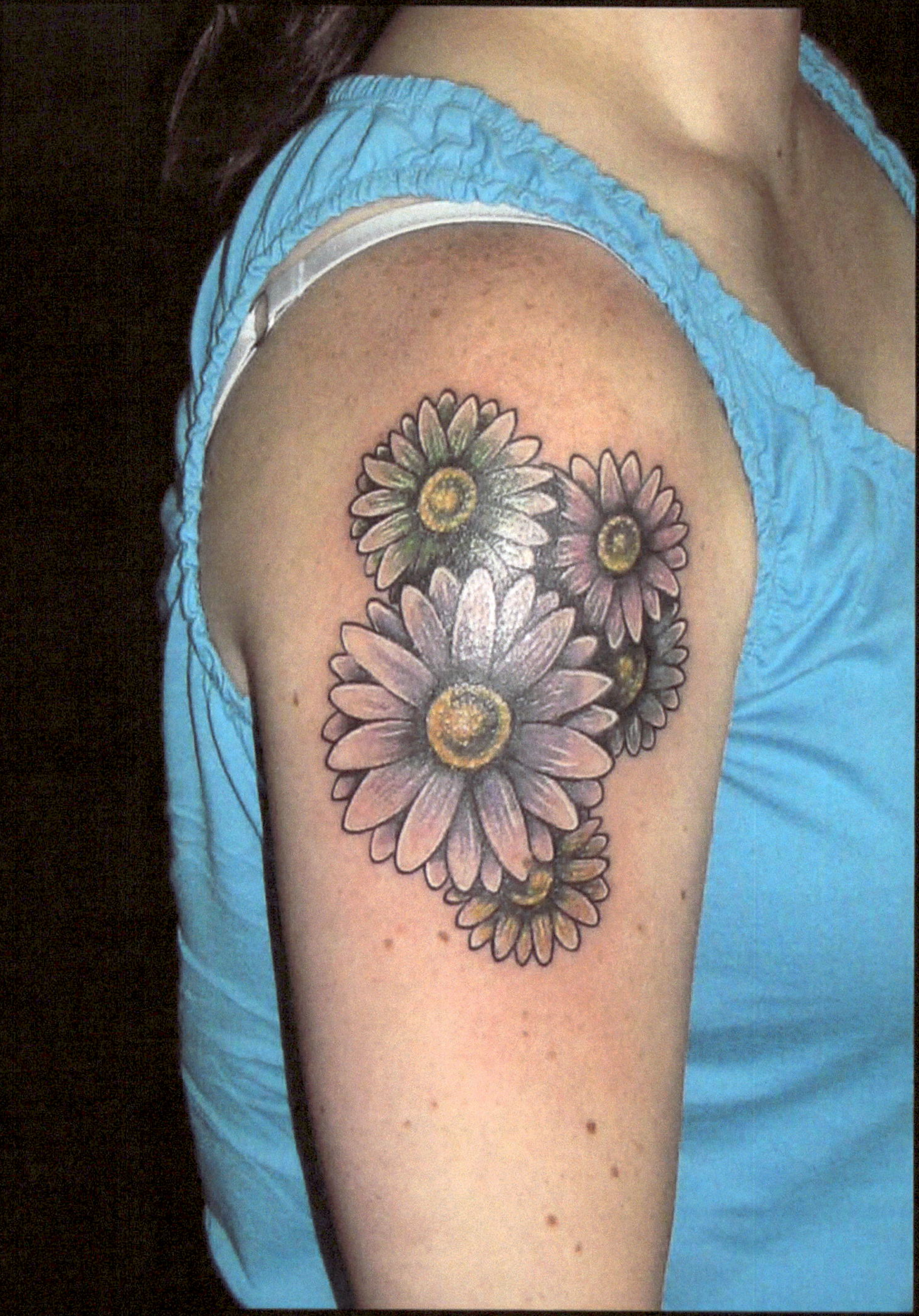

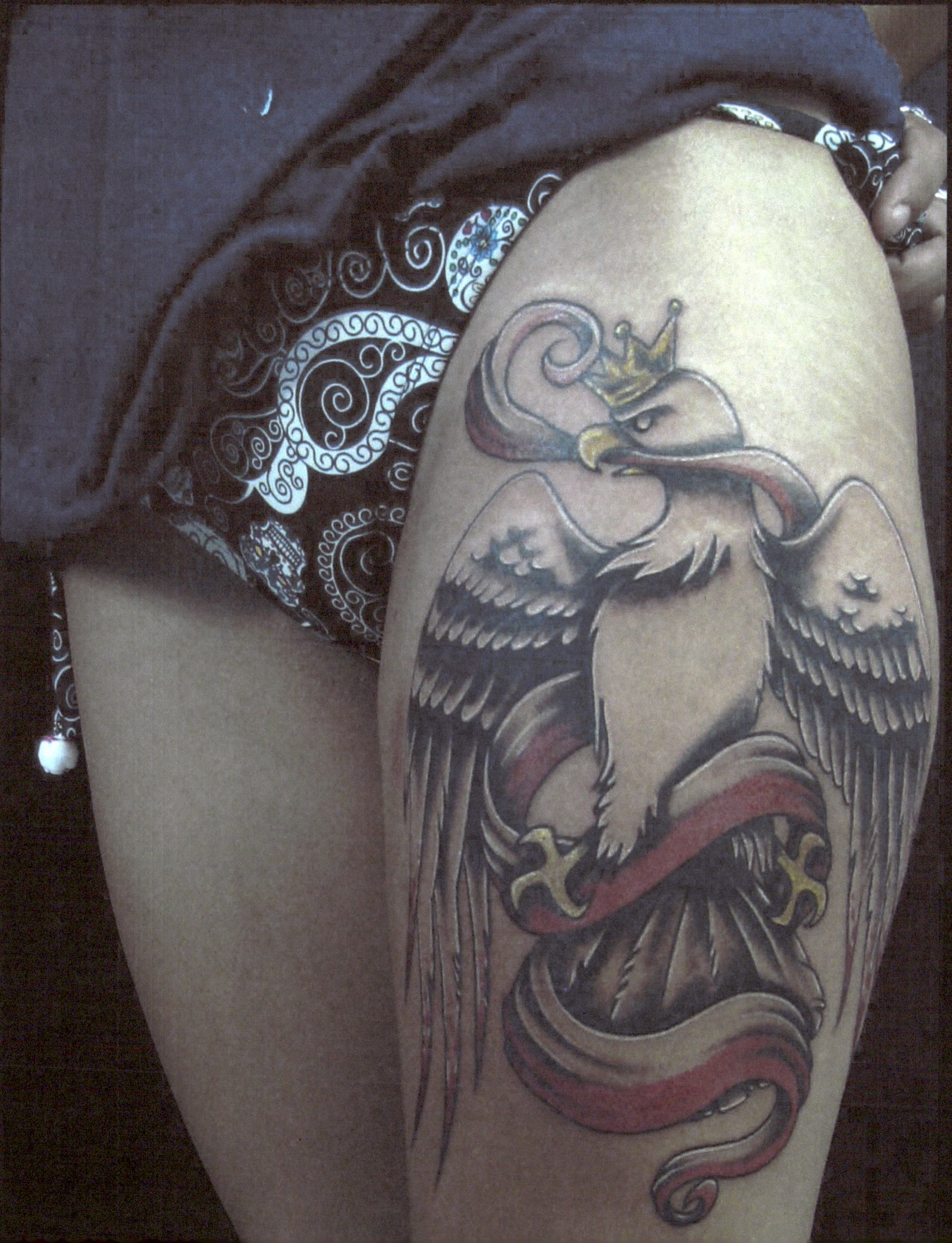

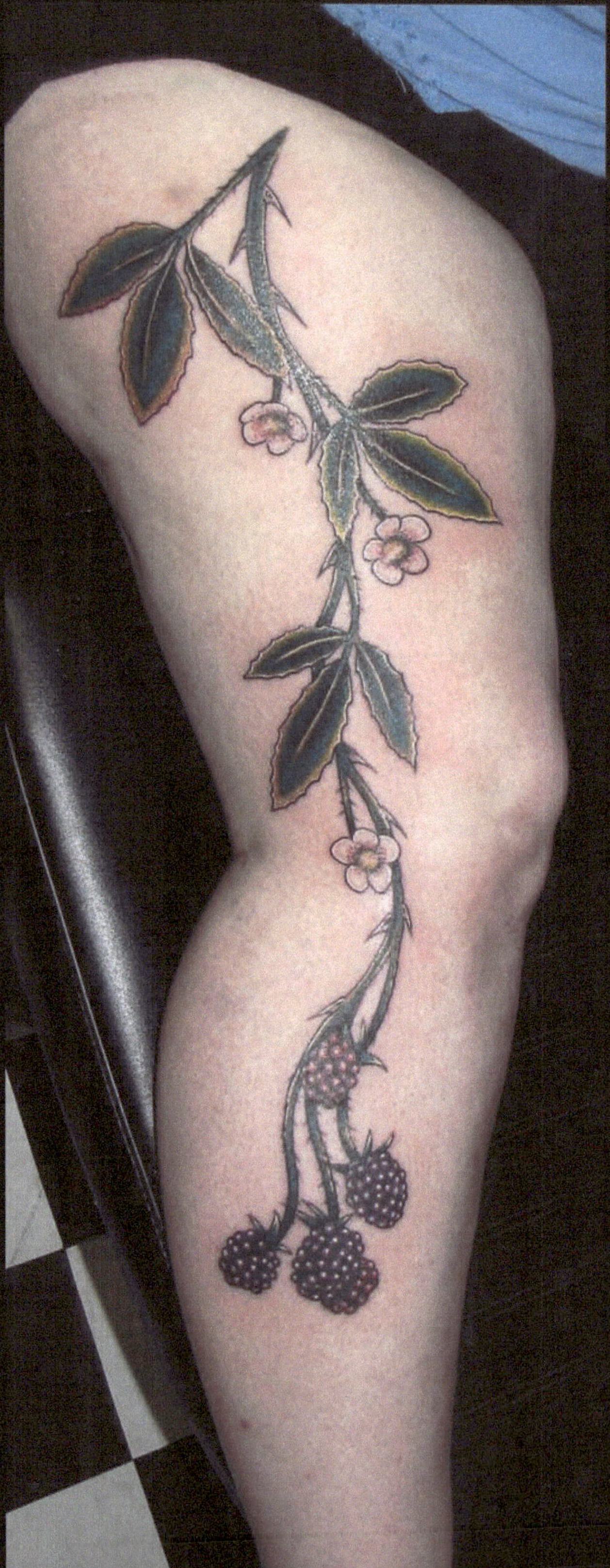

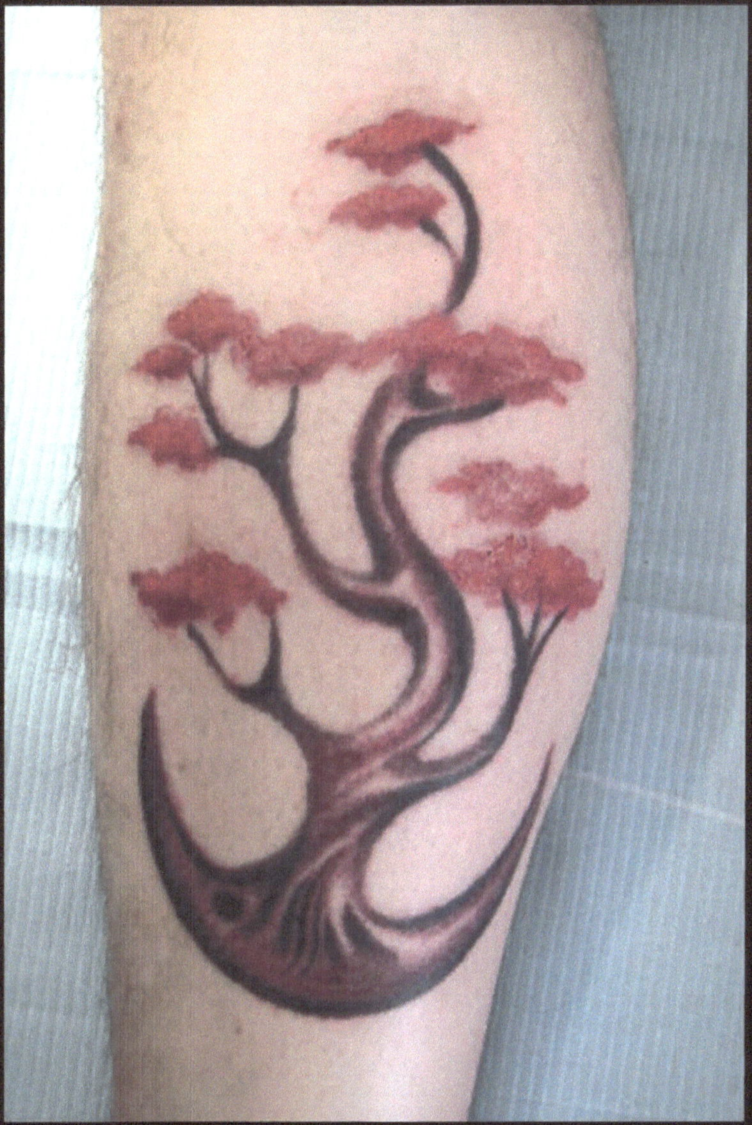

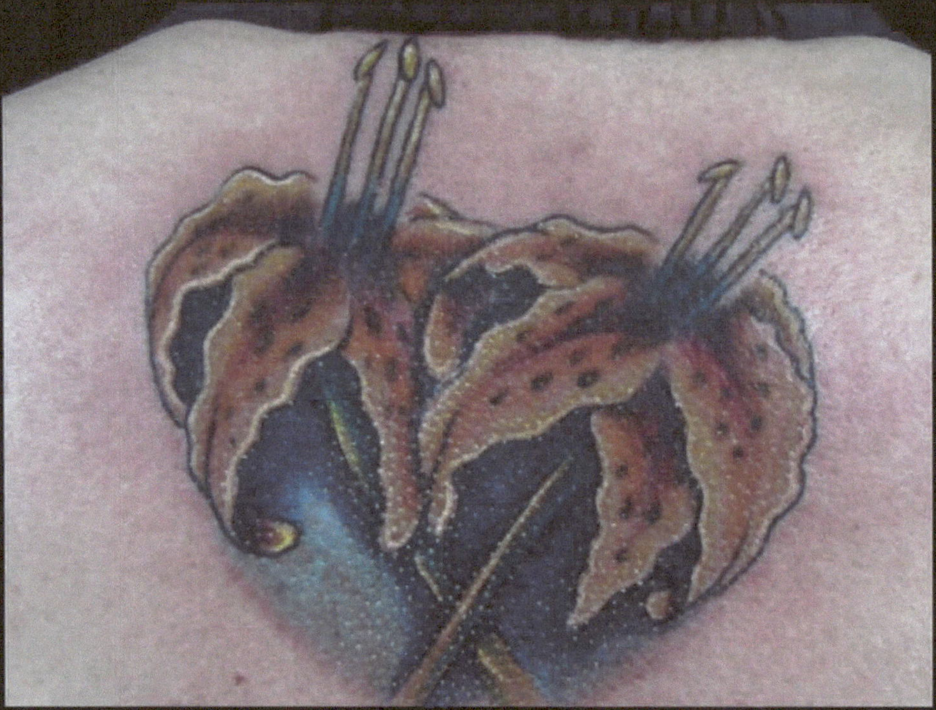

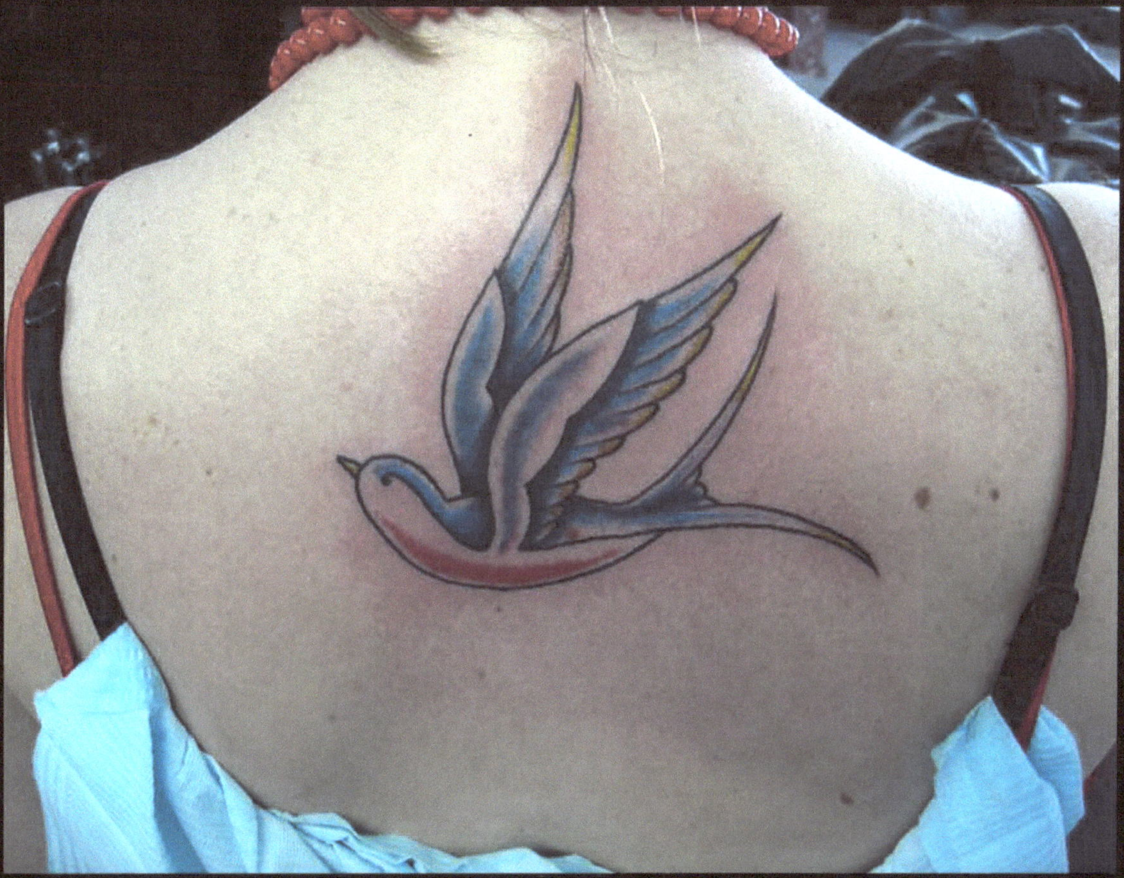

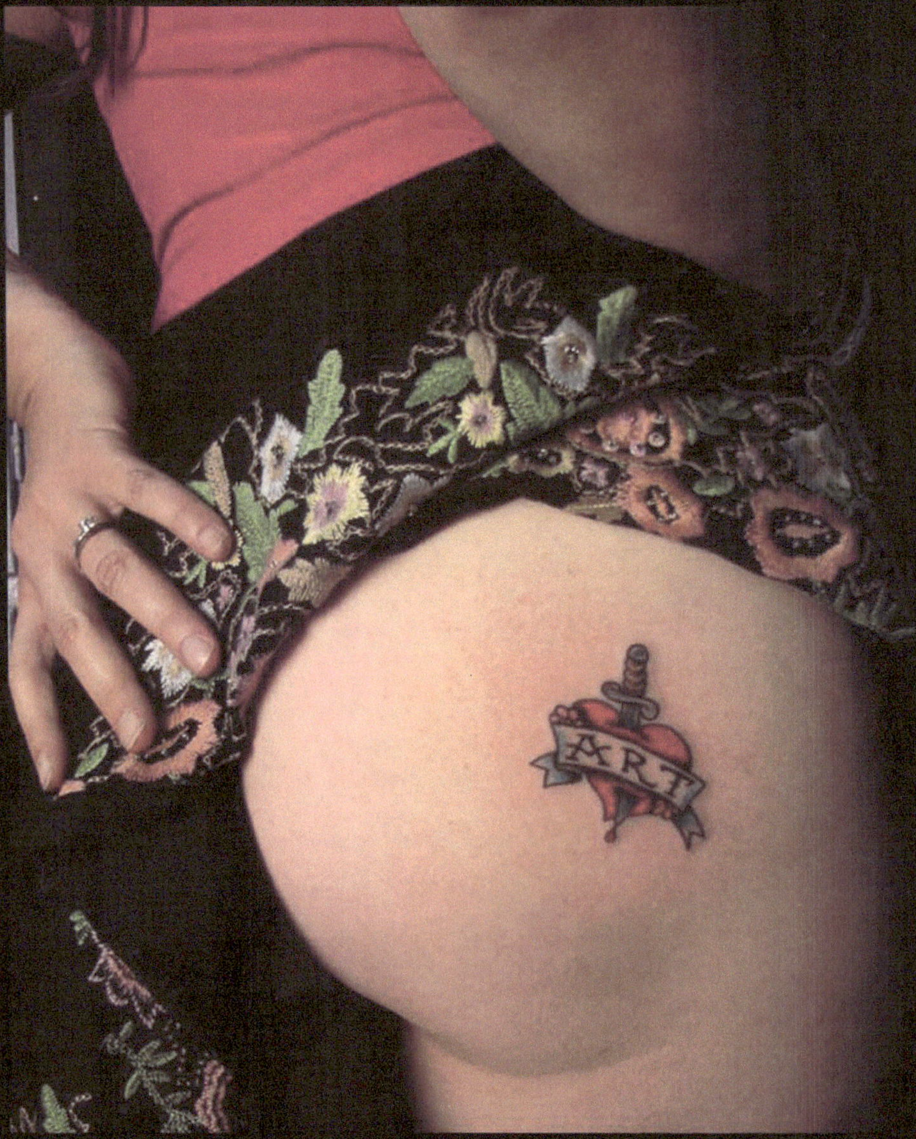
ART

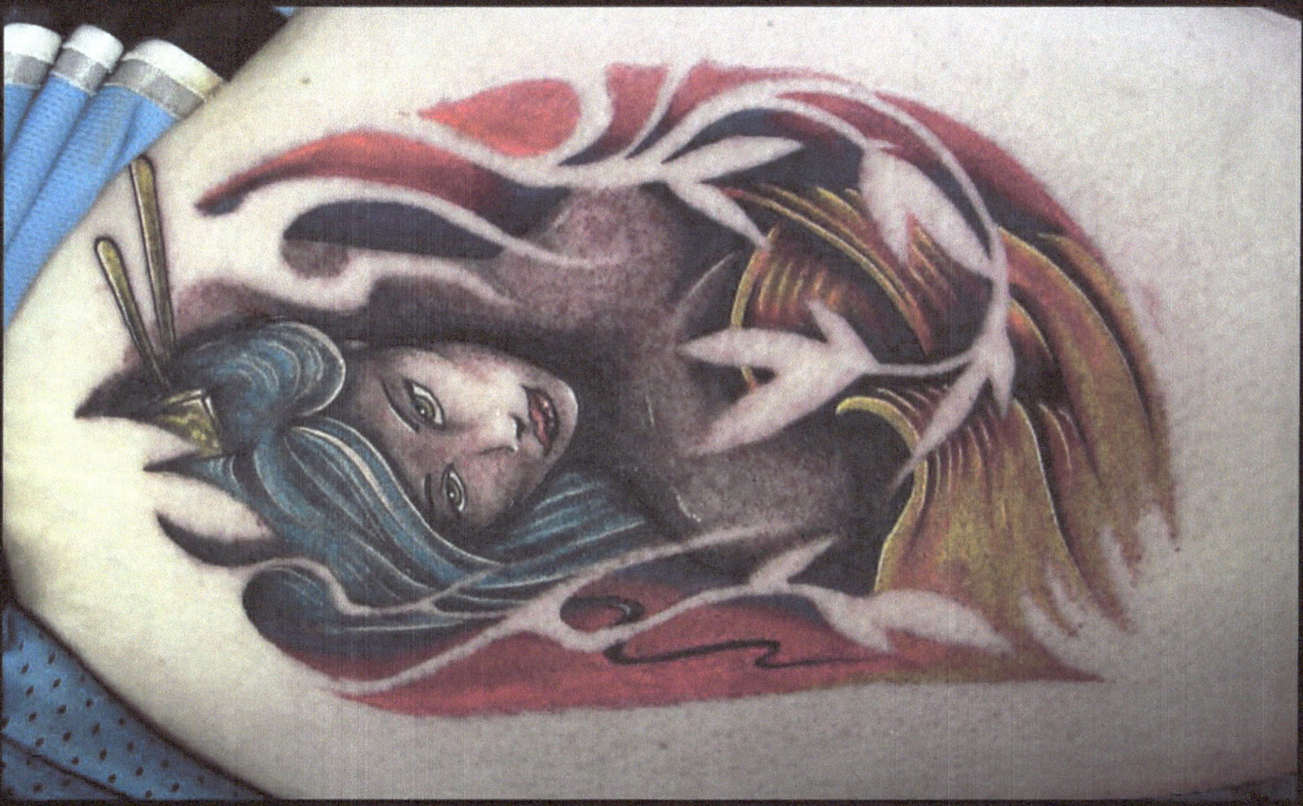

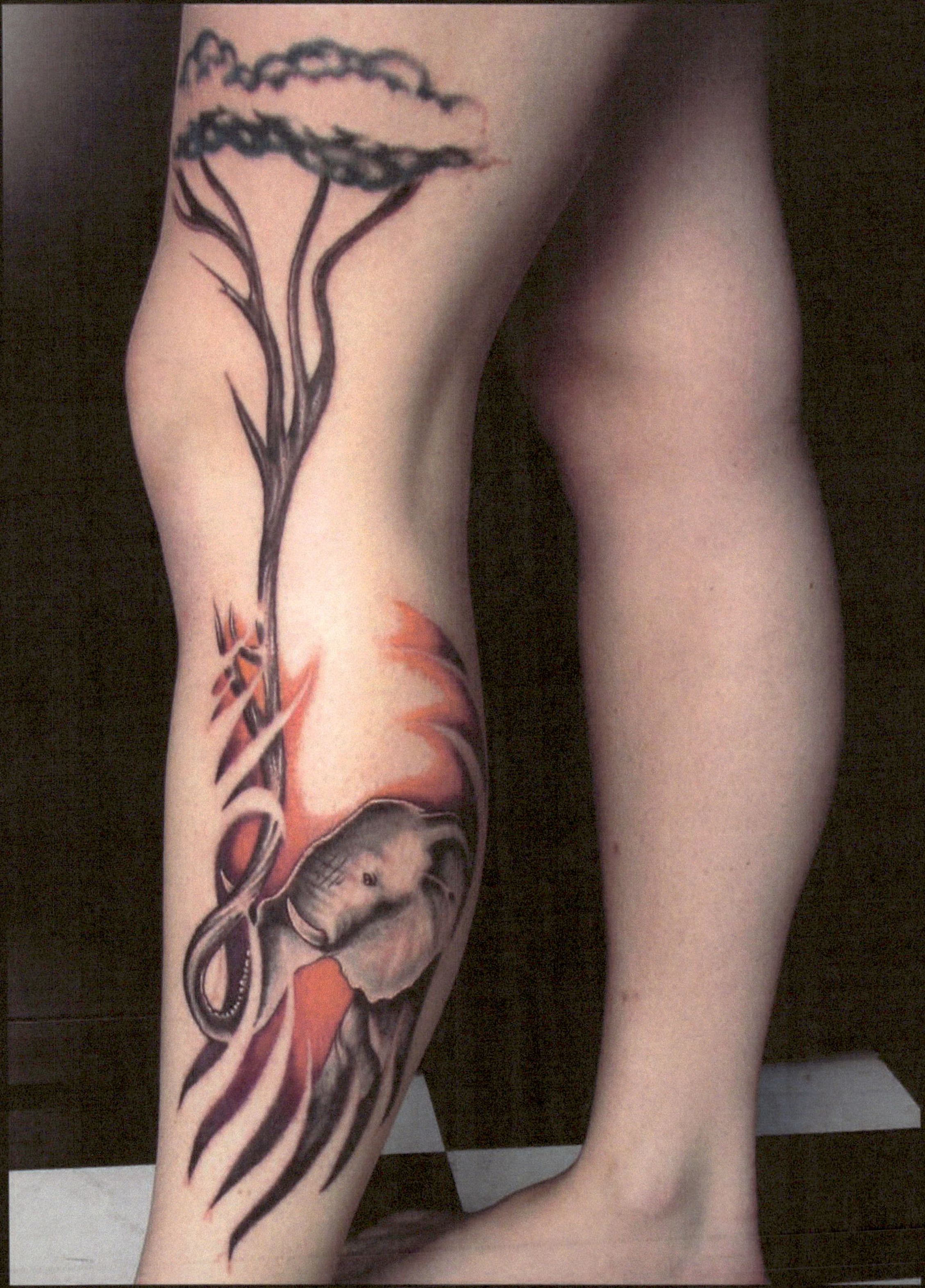

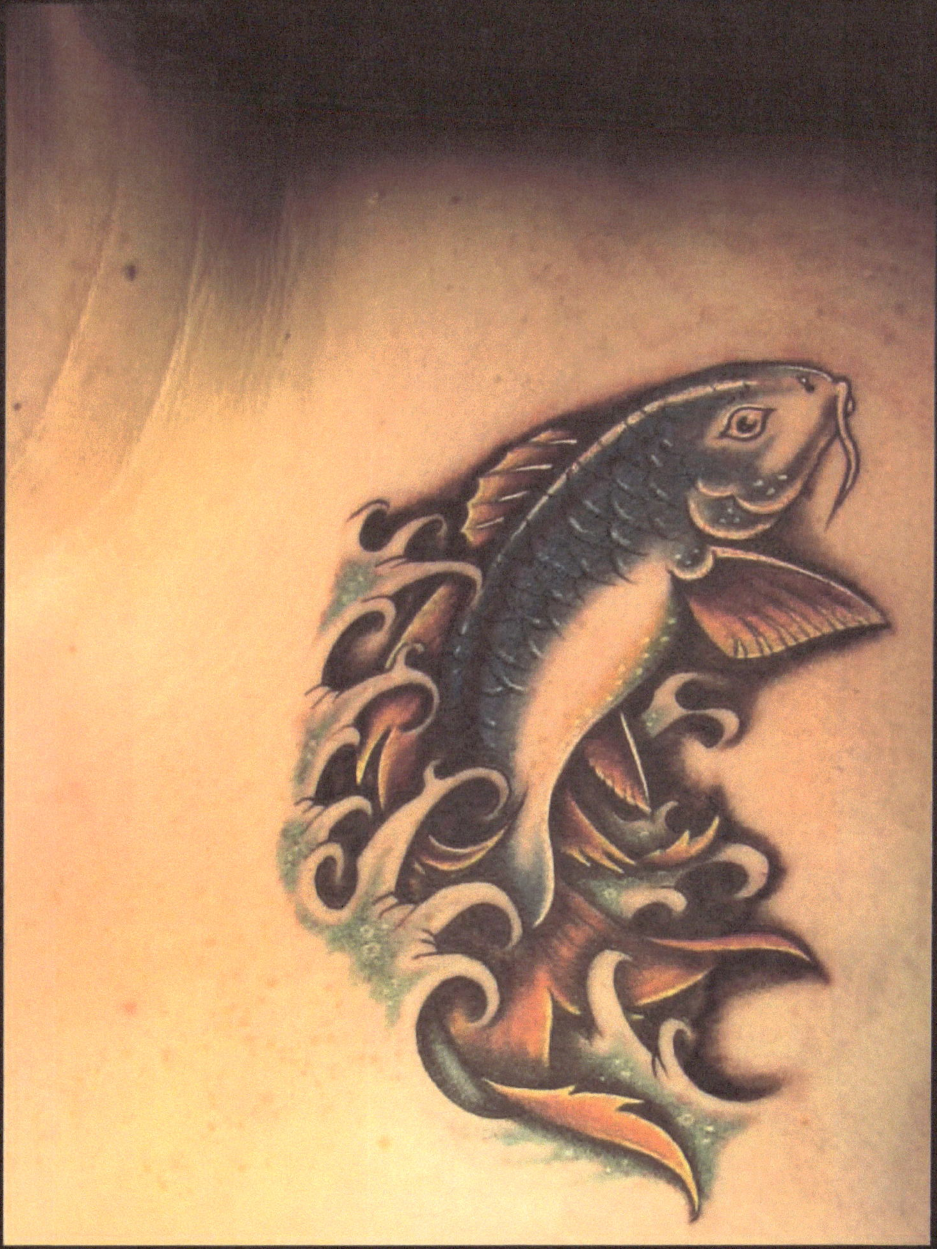

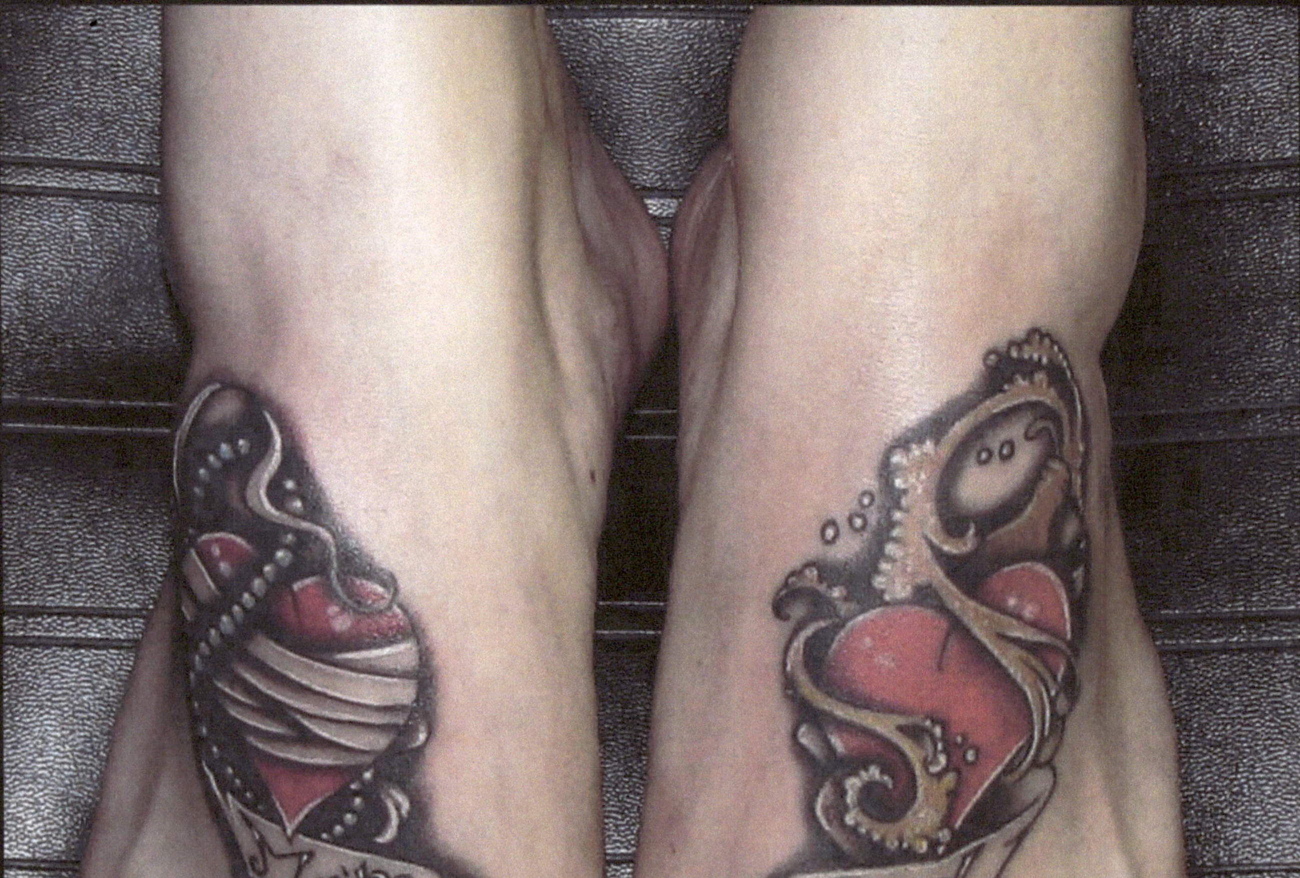
Mom
Dad

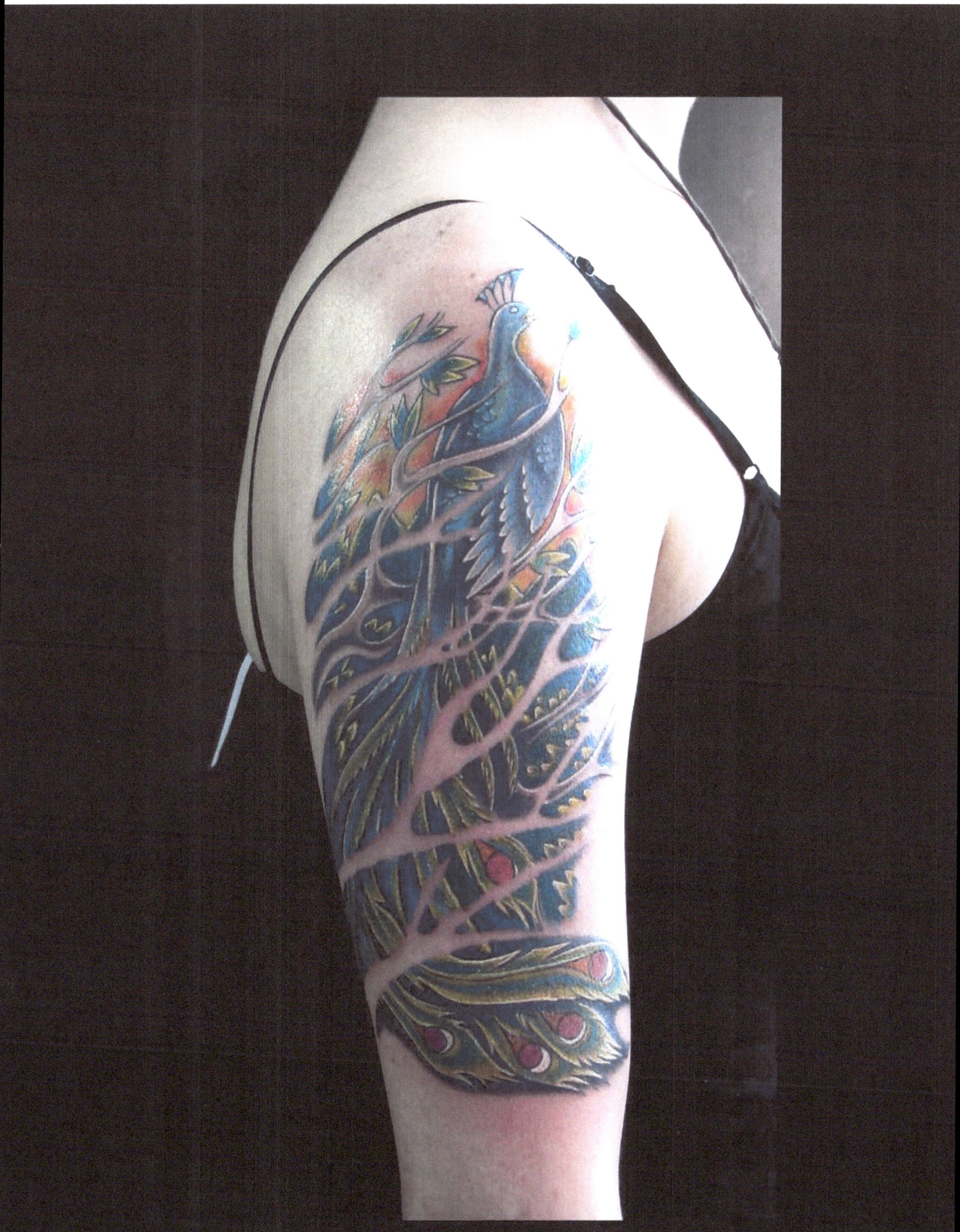

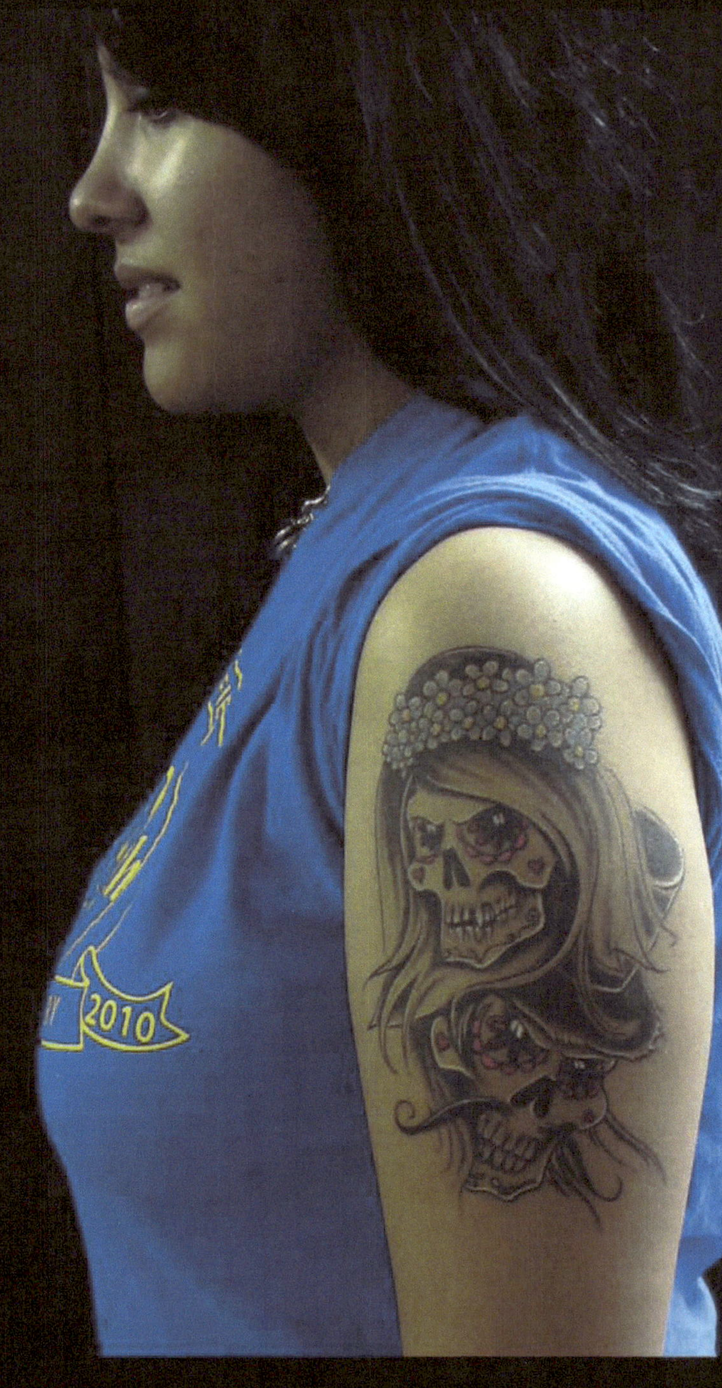
2010

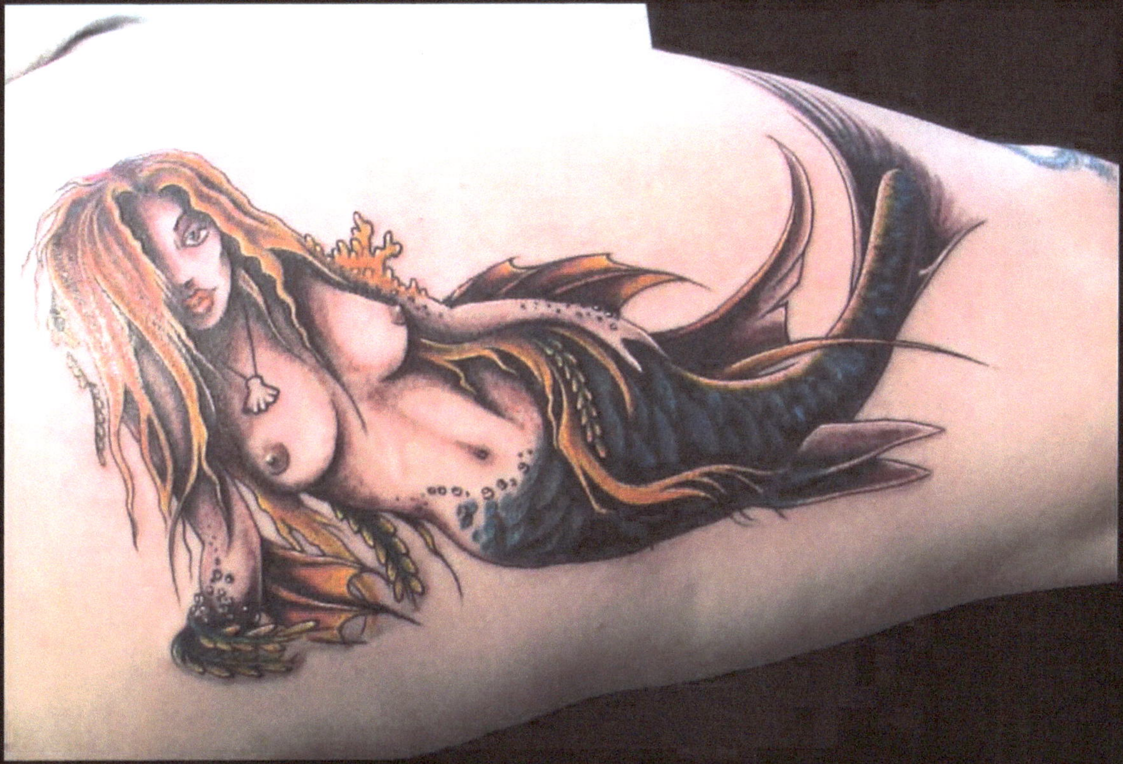

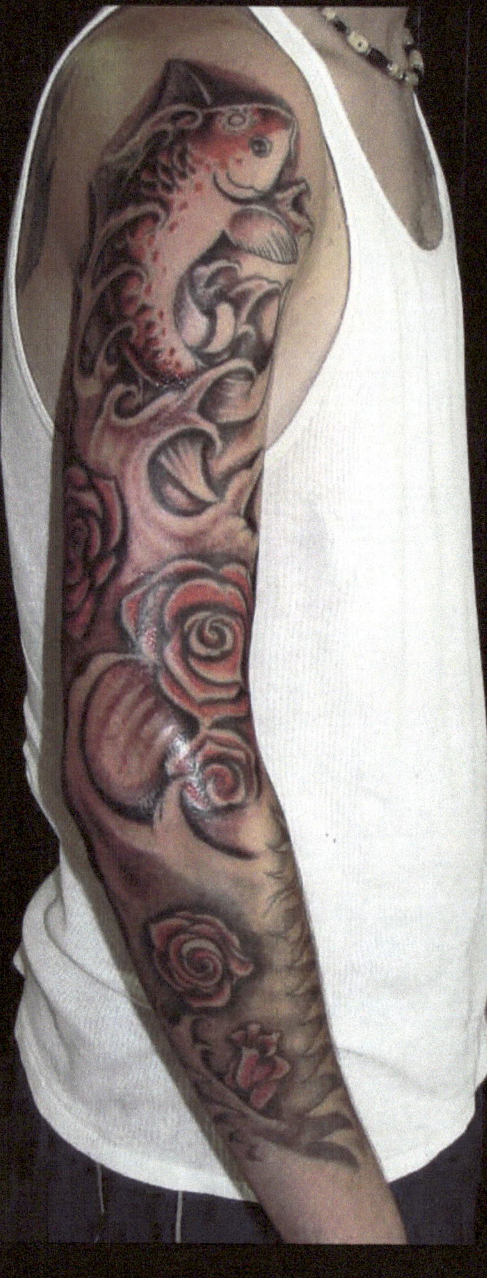

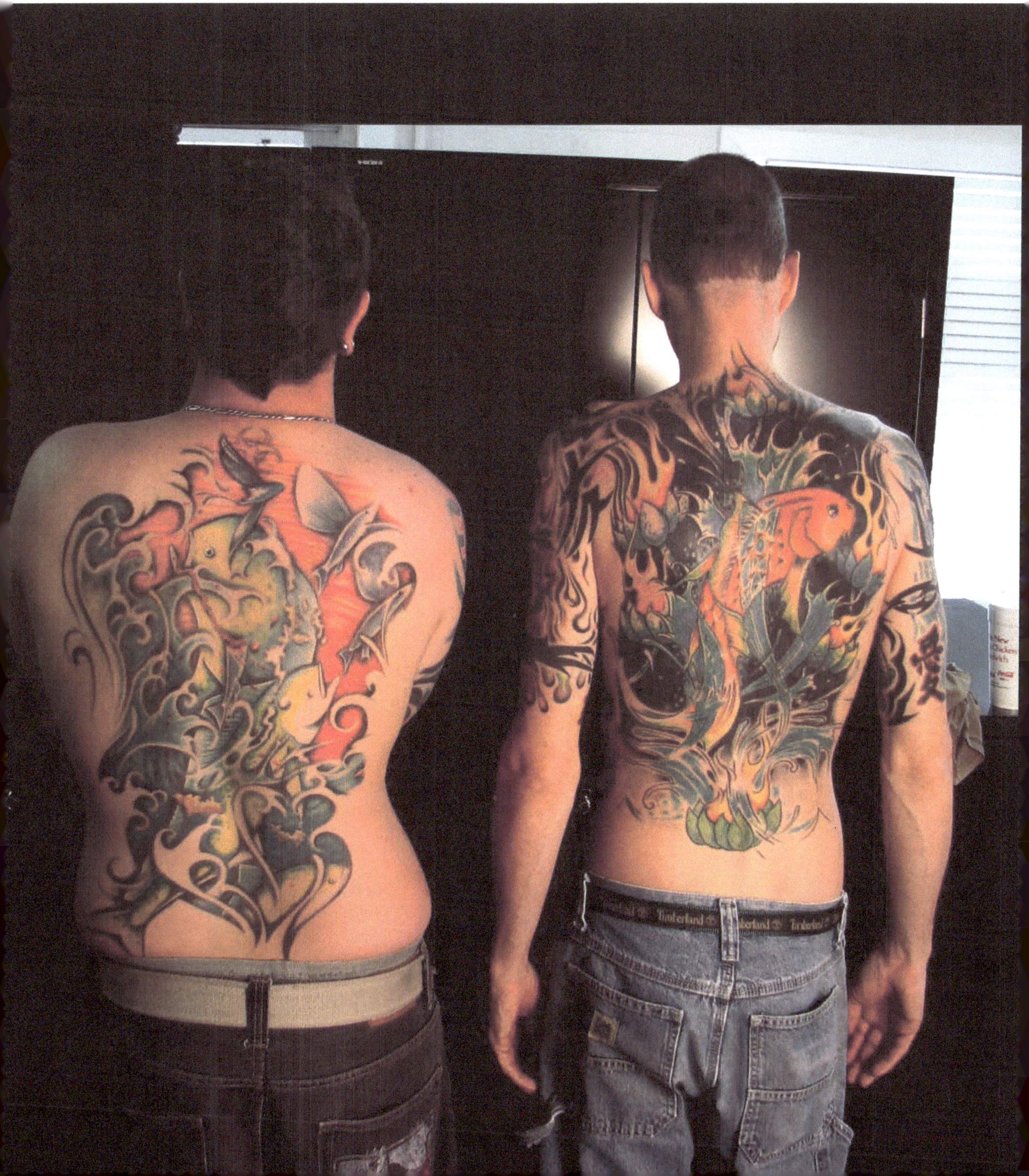
Timberland

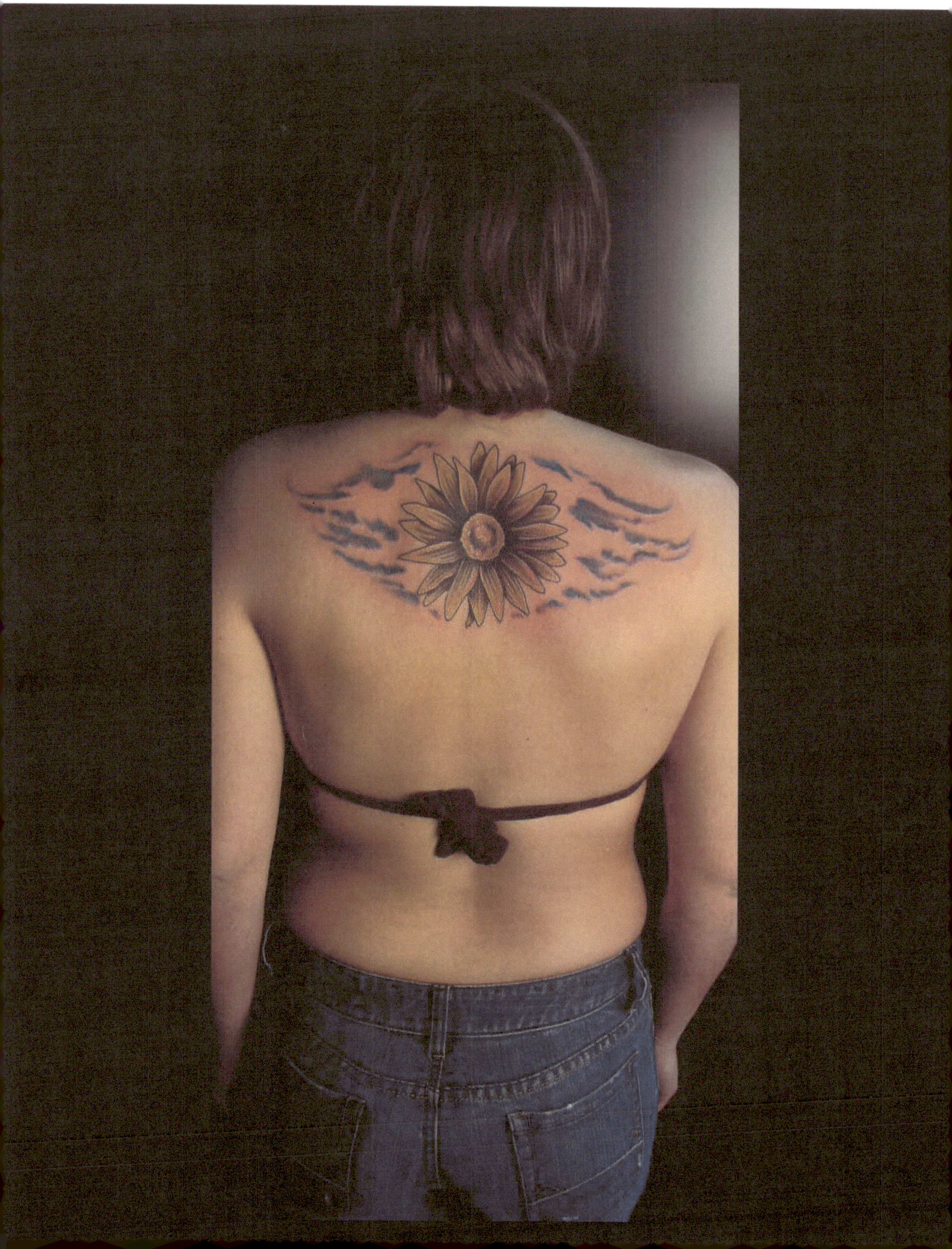

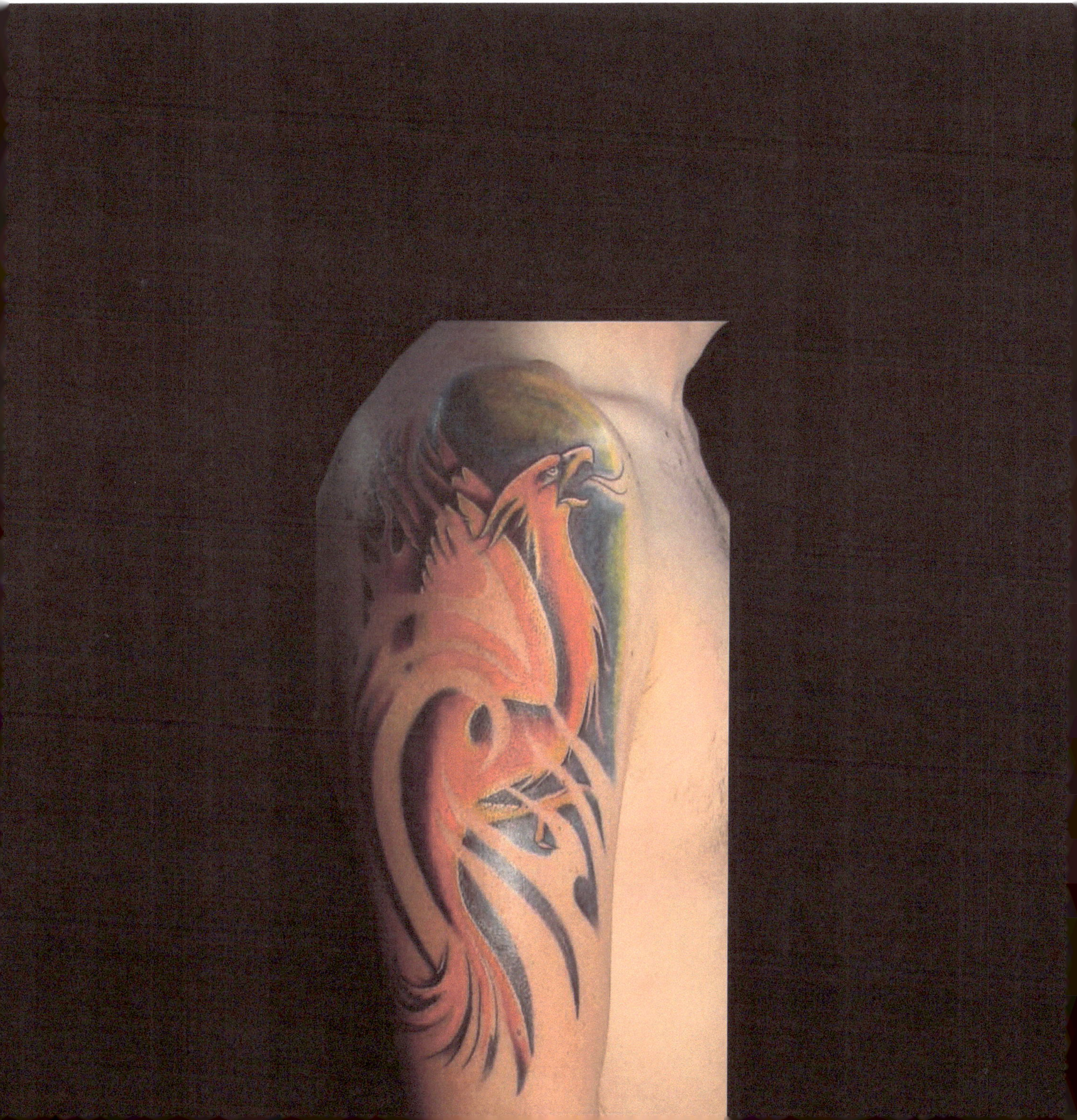

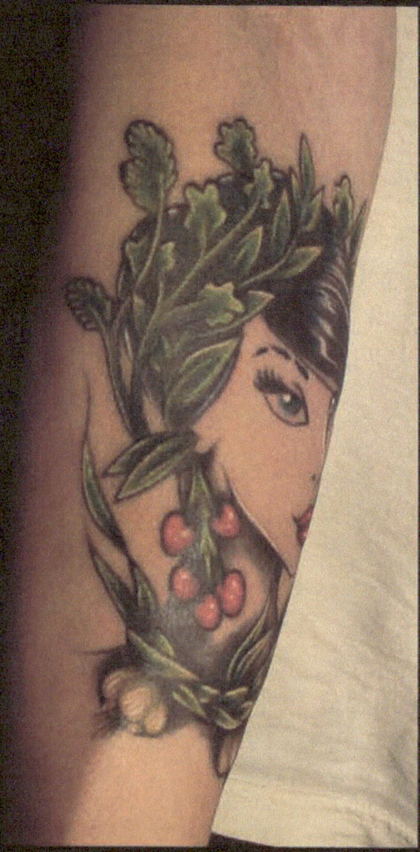
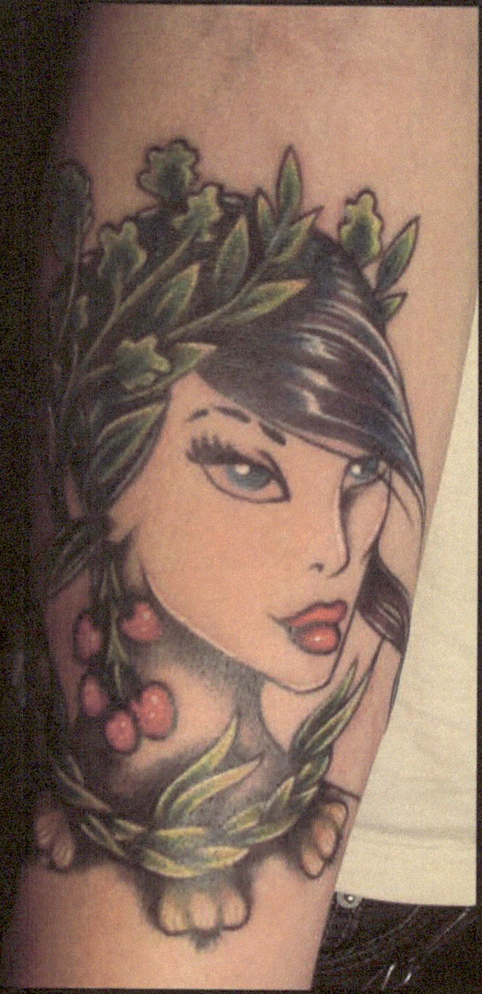
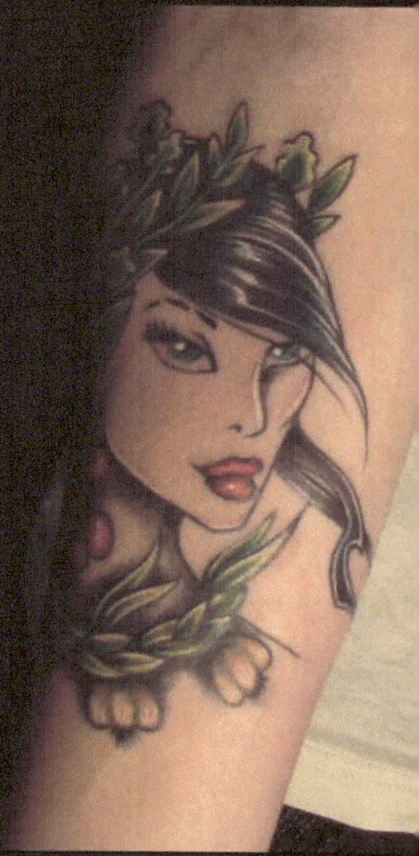

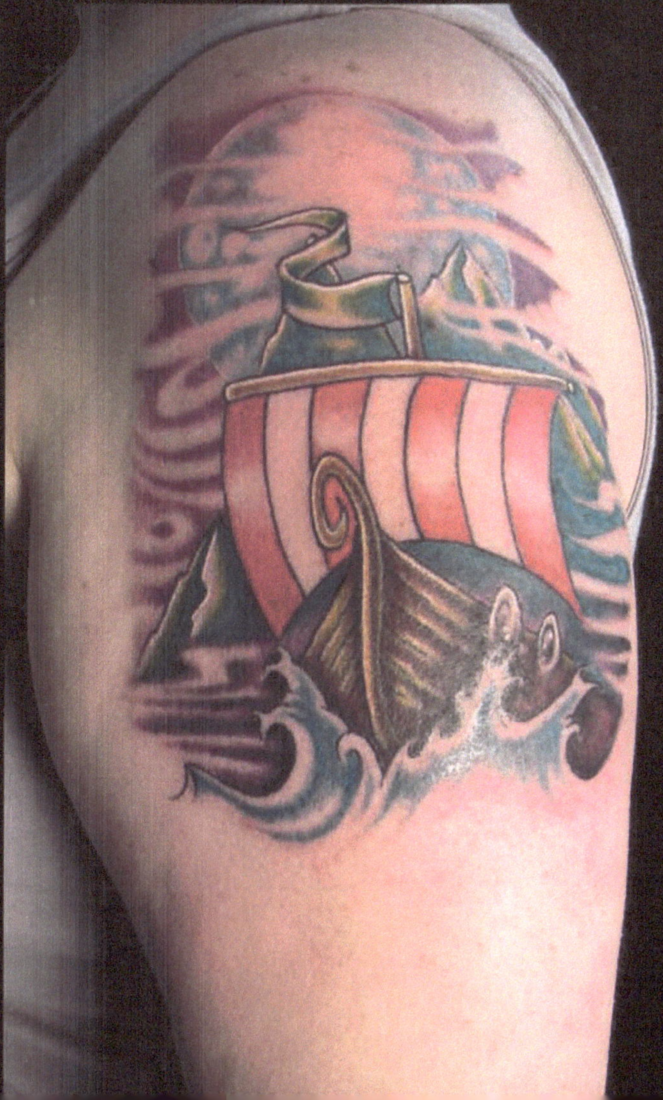

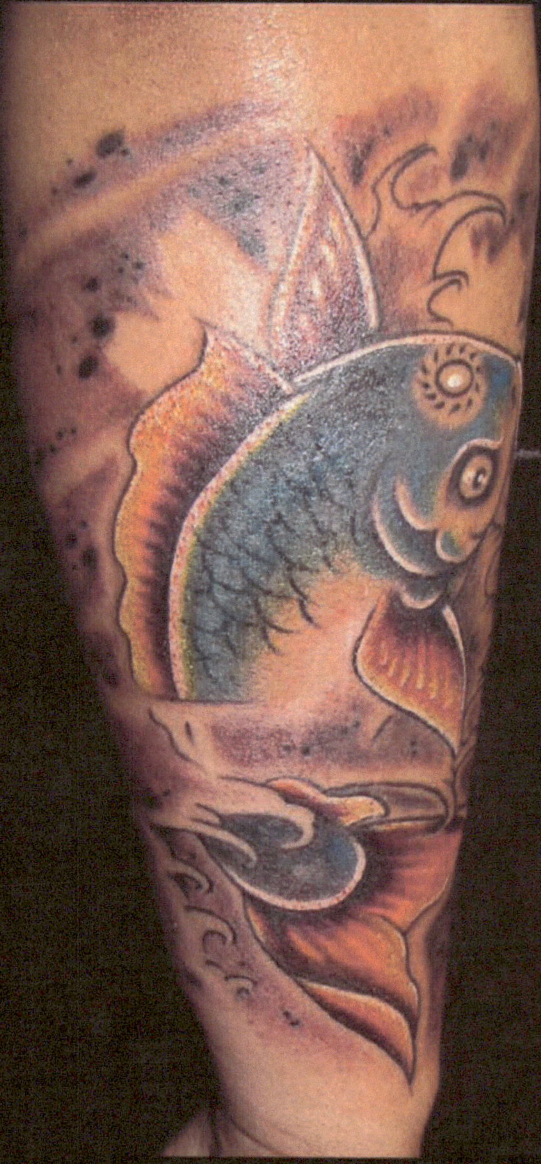

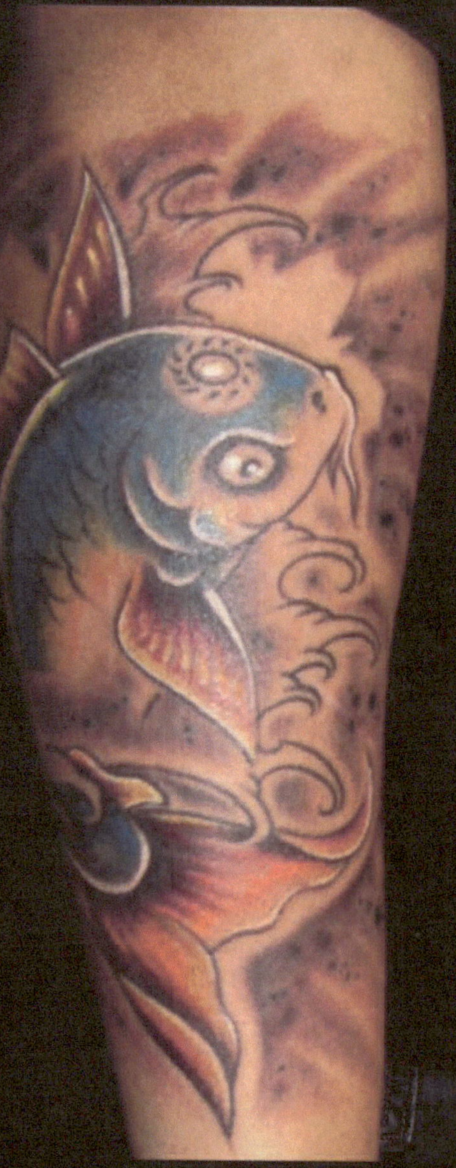

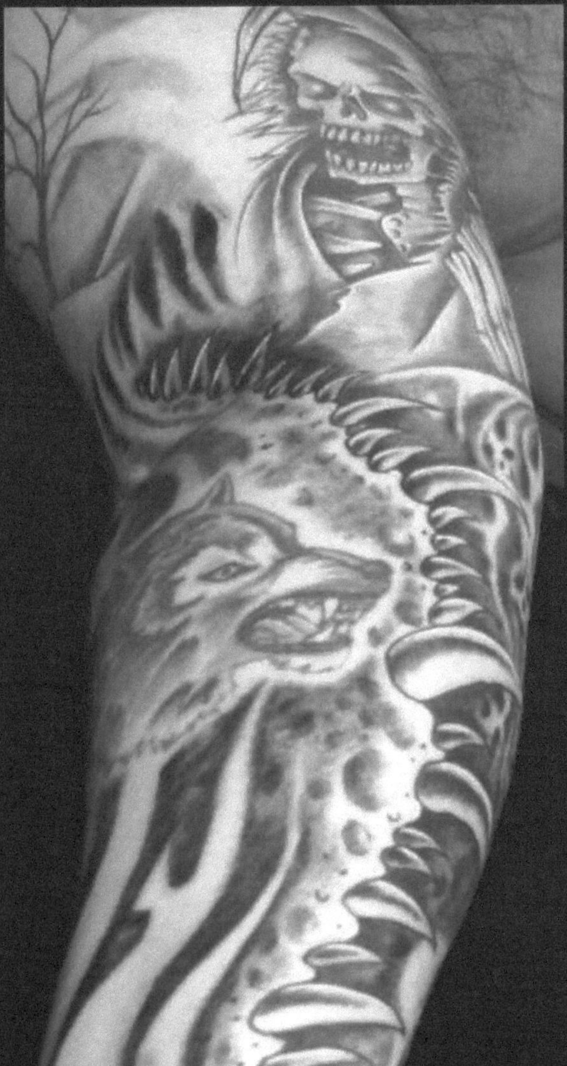

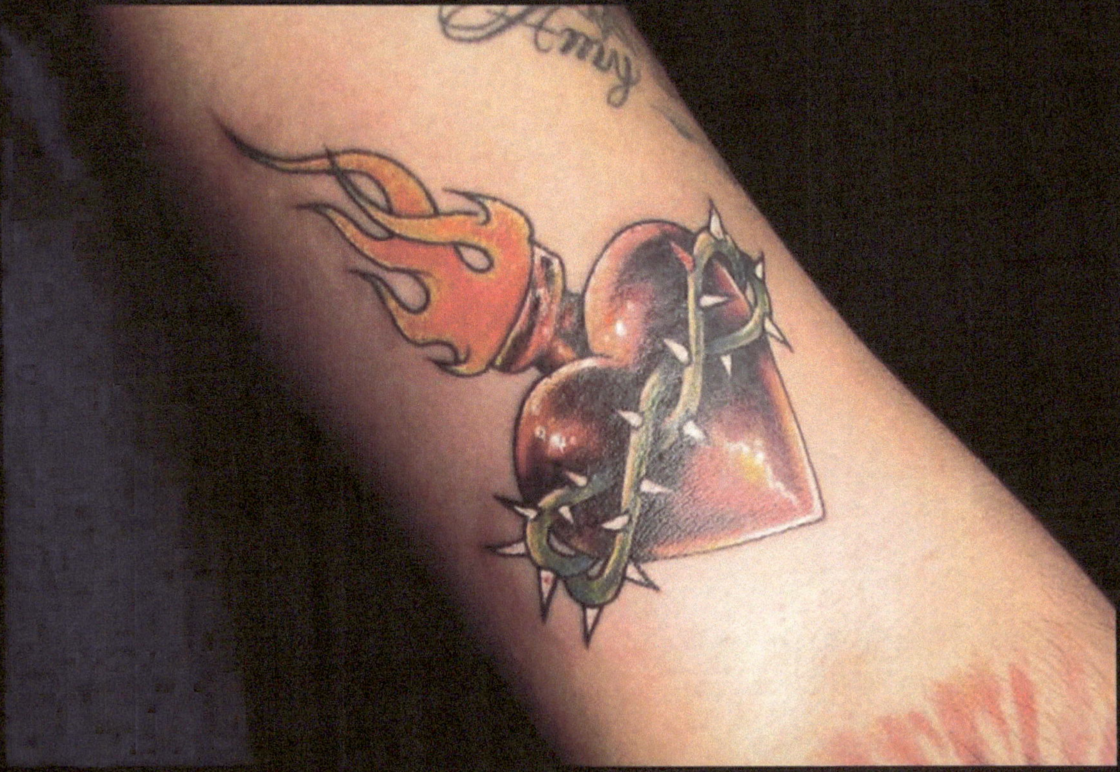

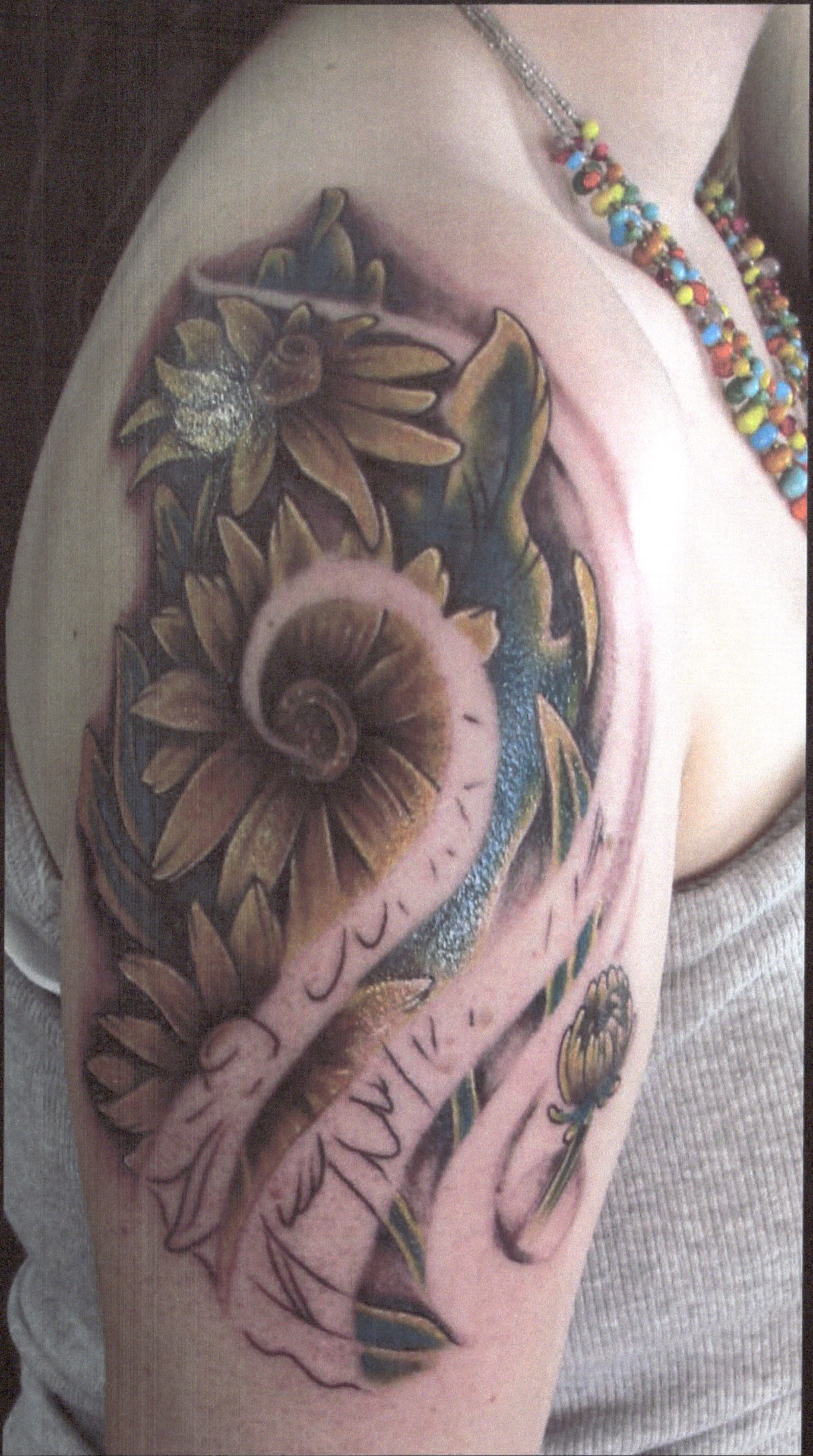

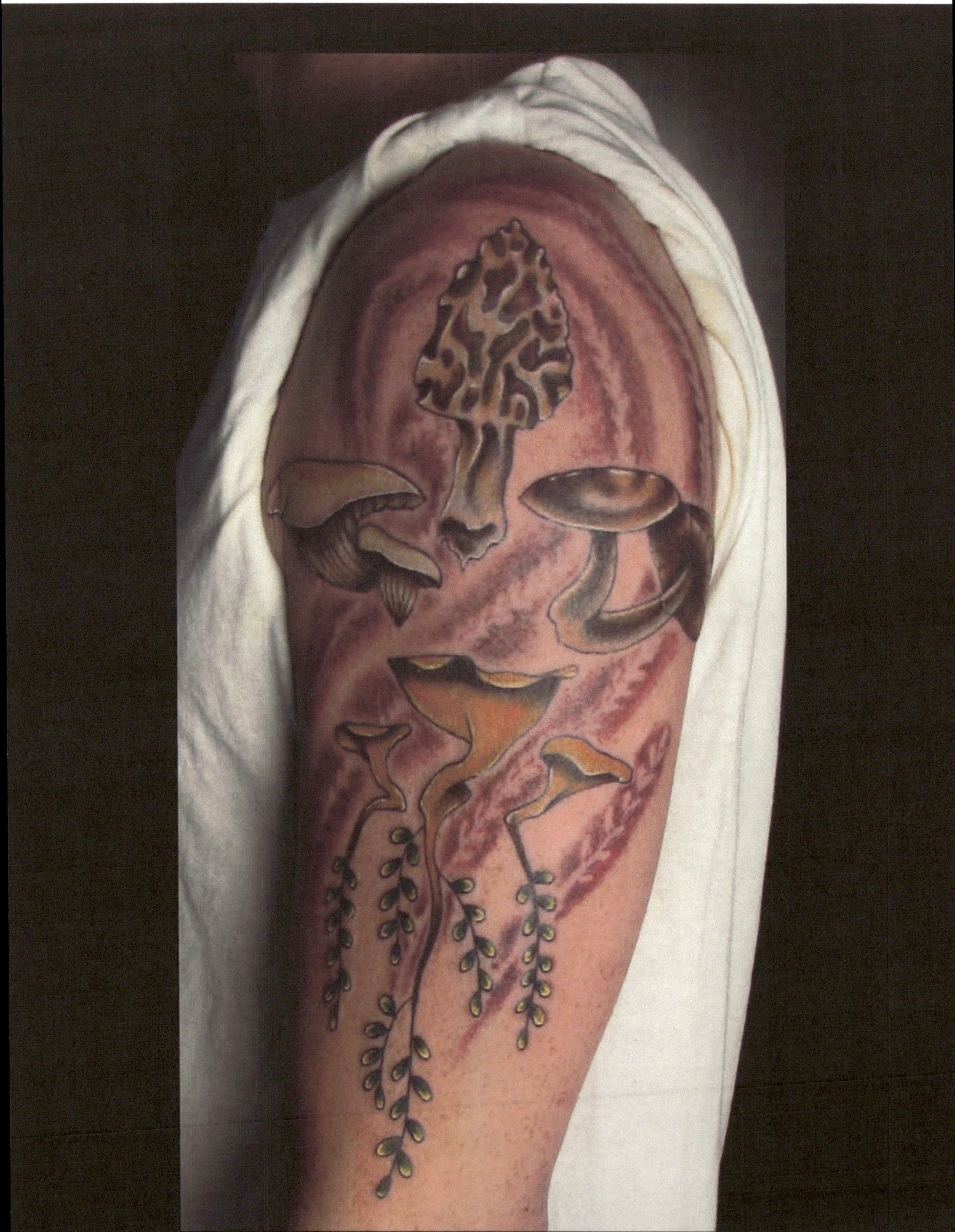

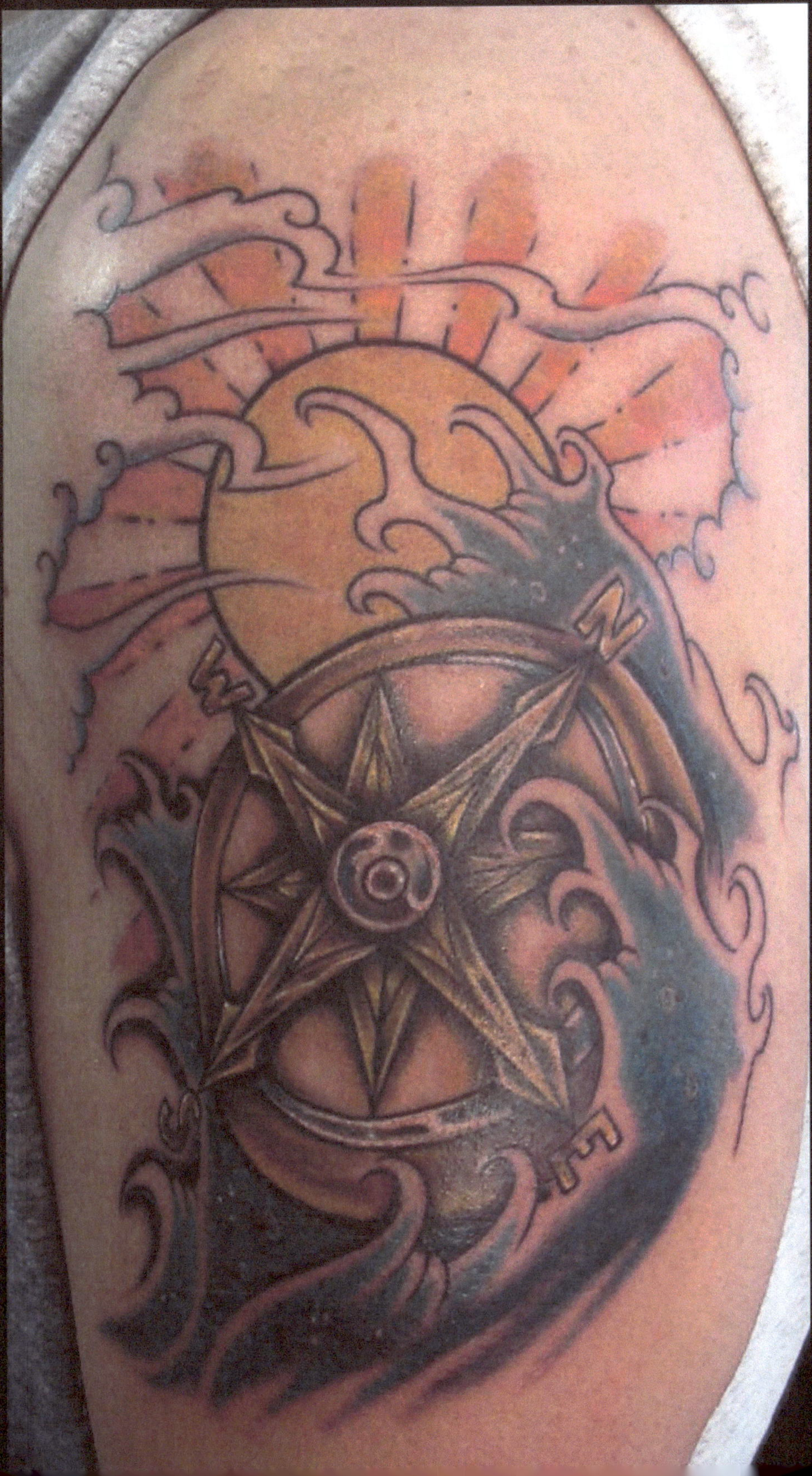
W
N
E

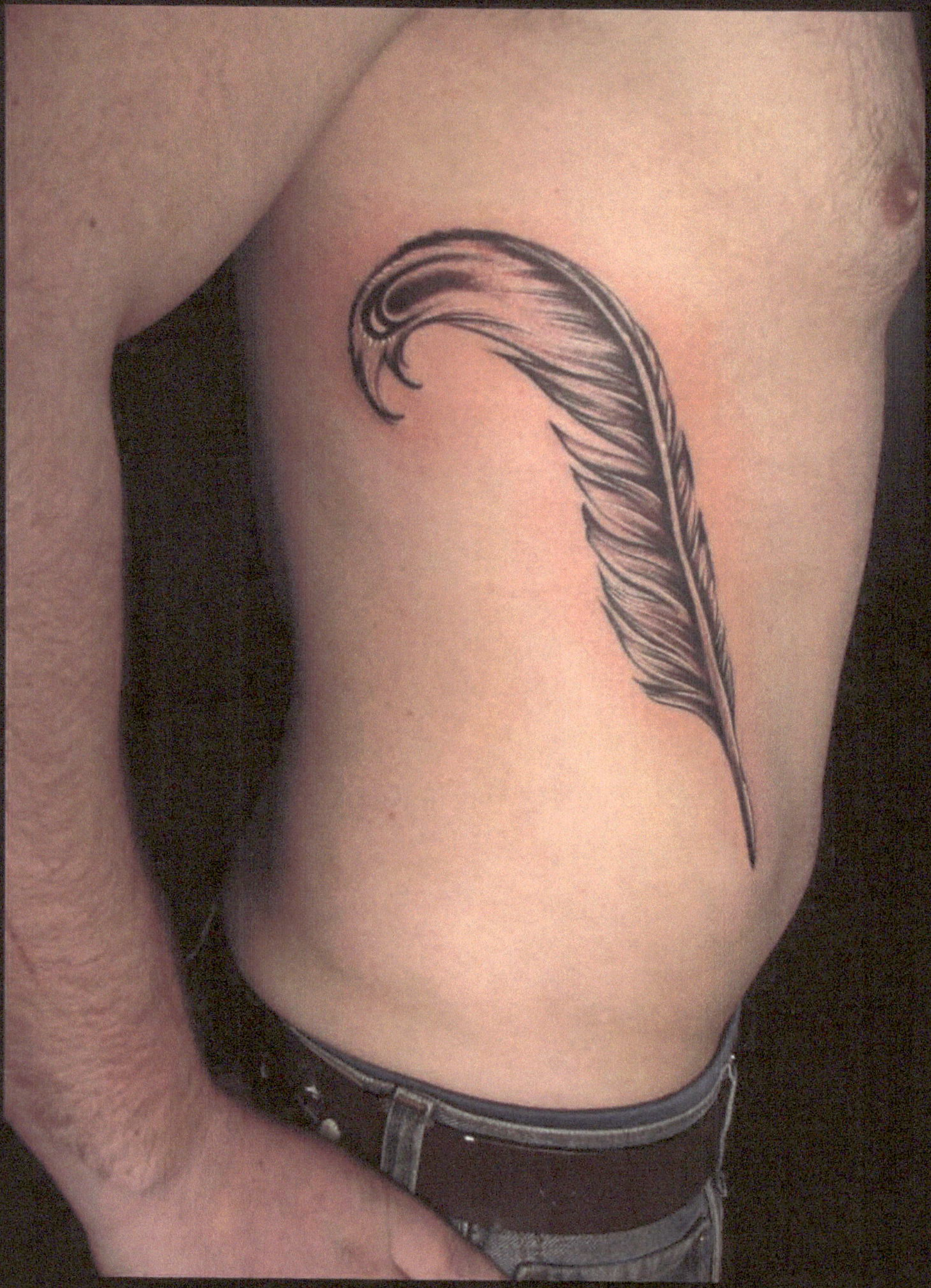

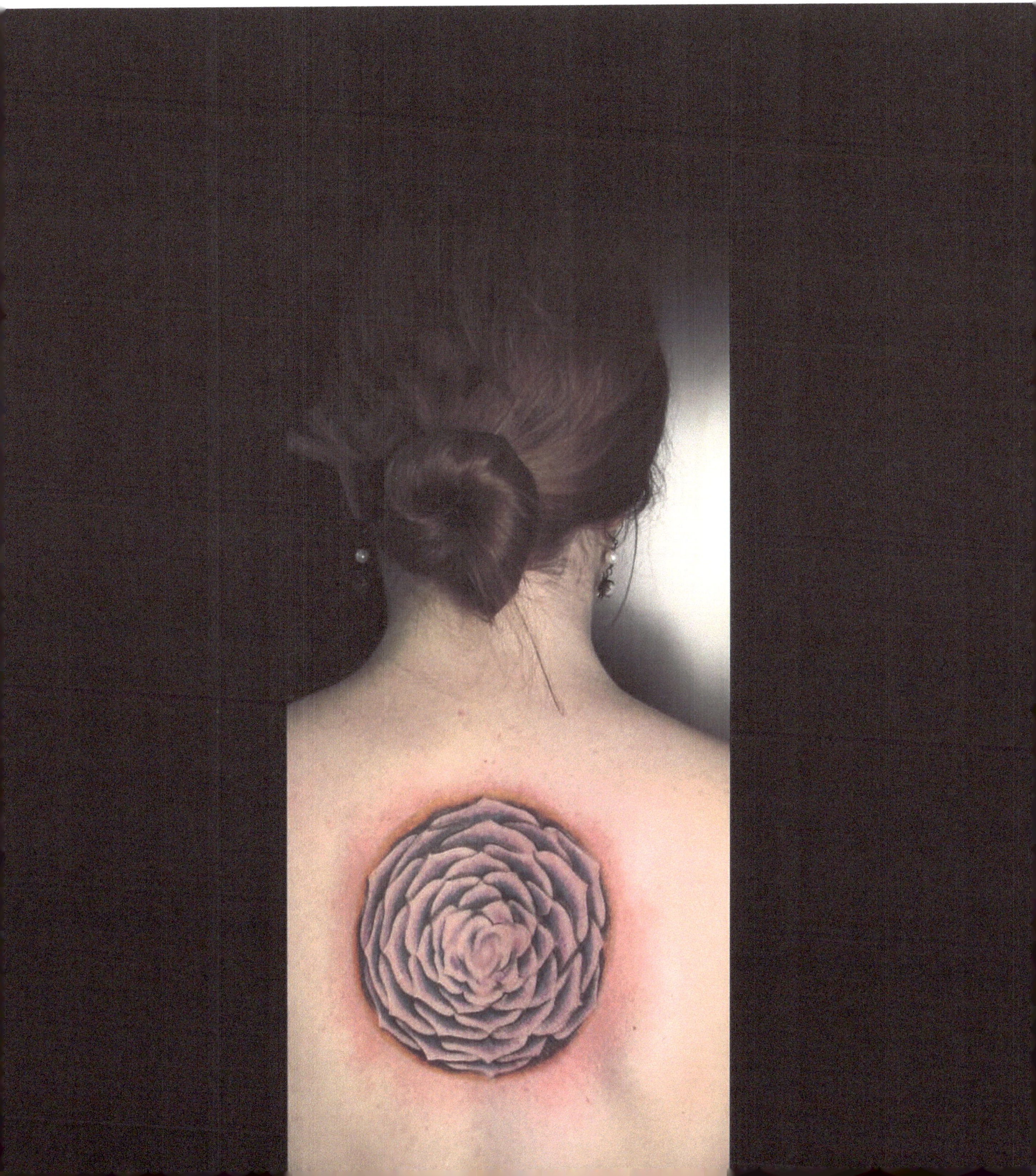

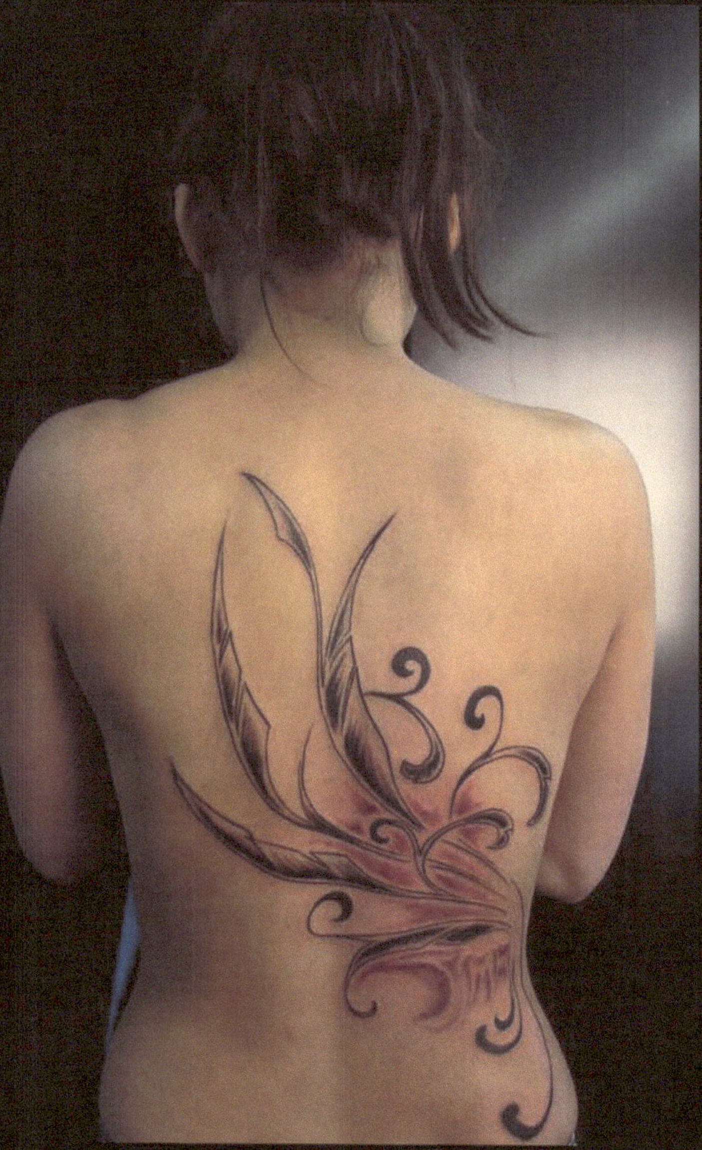

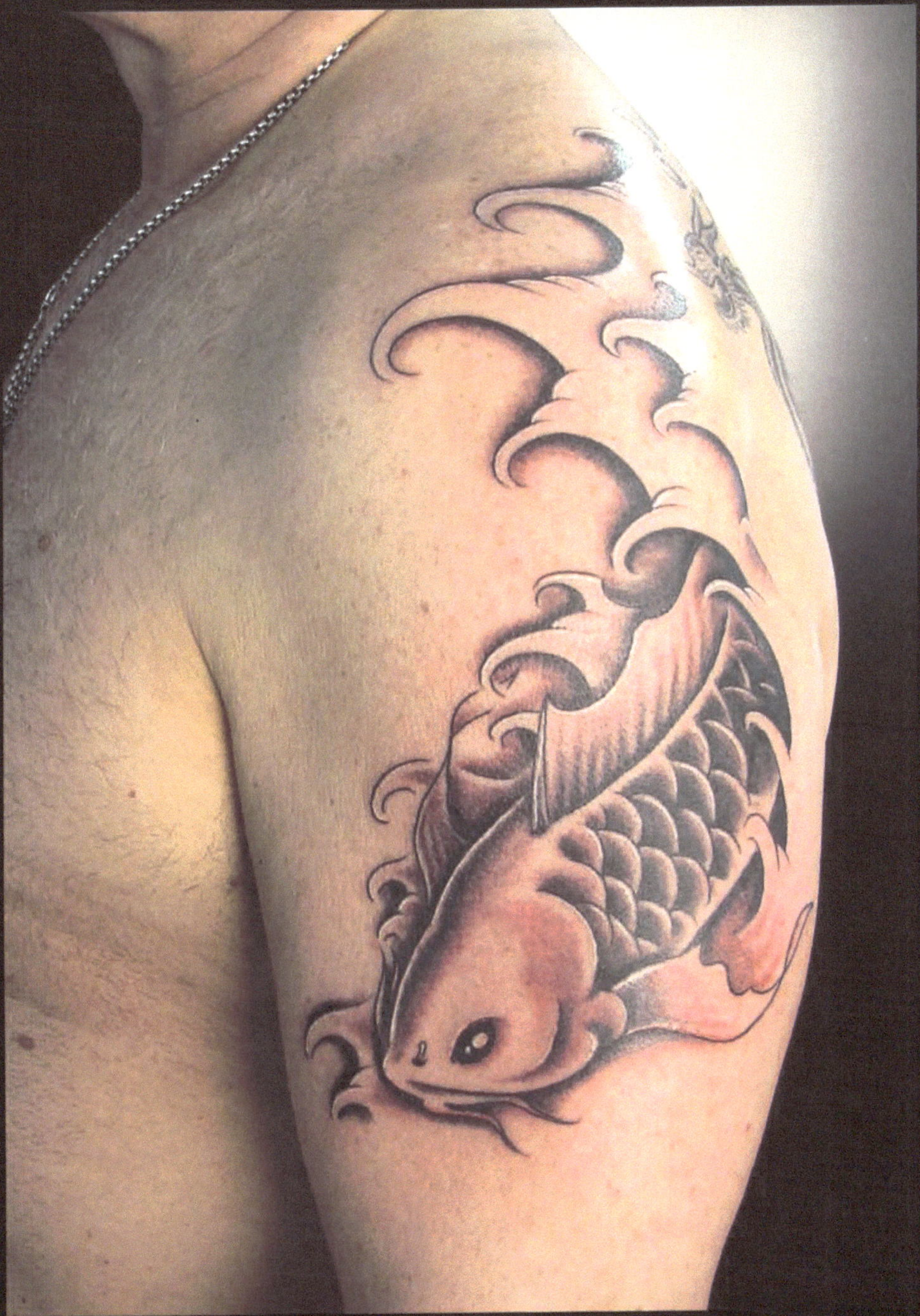

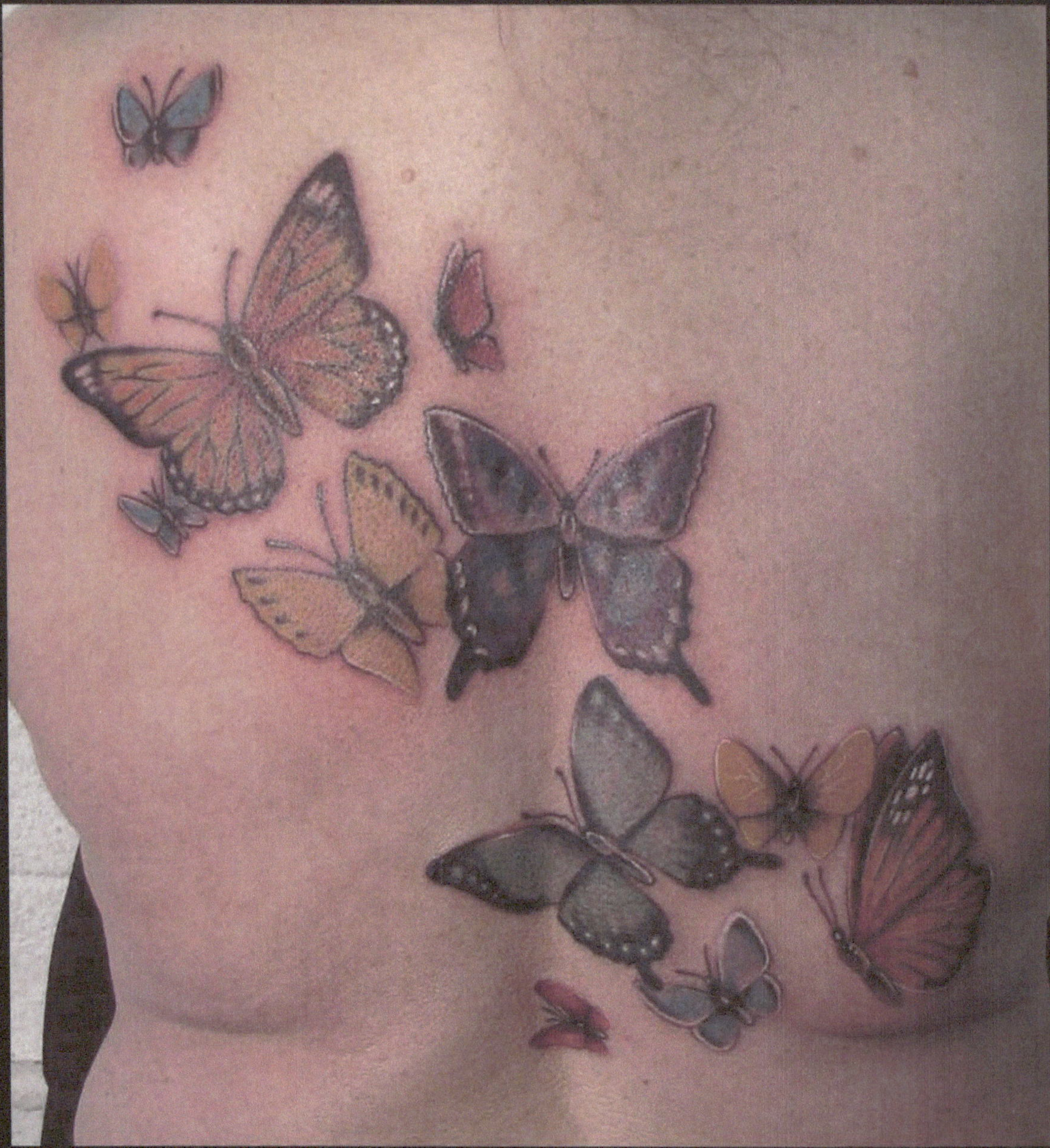

www.ingramcontent.com/pod-product-compliance
Lightning Source LLC
Chambersburg PA
CBHW050733180526
45159CB00003B/1213